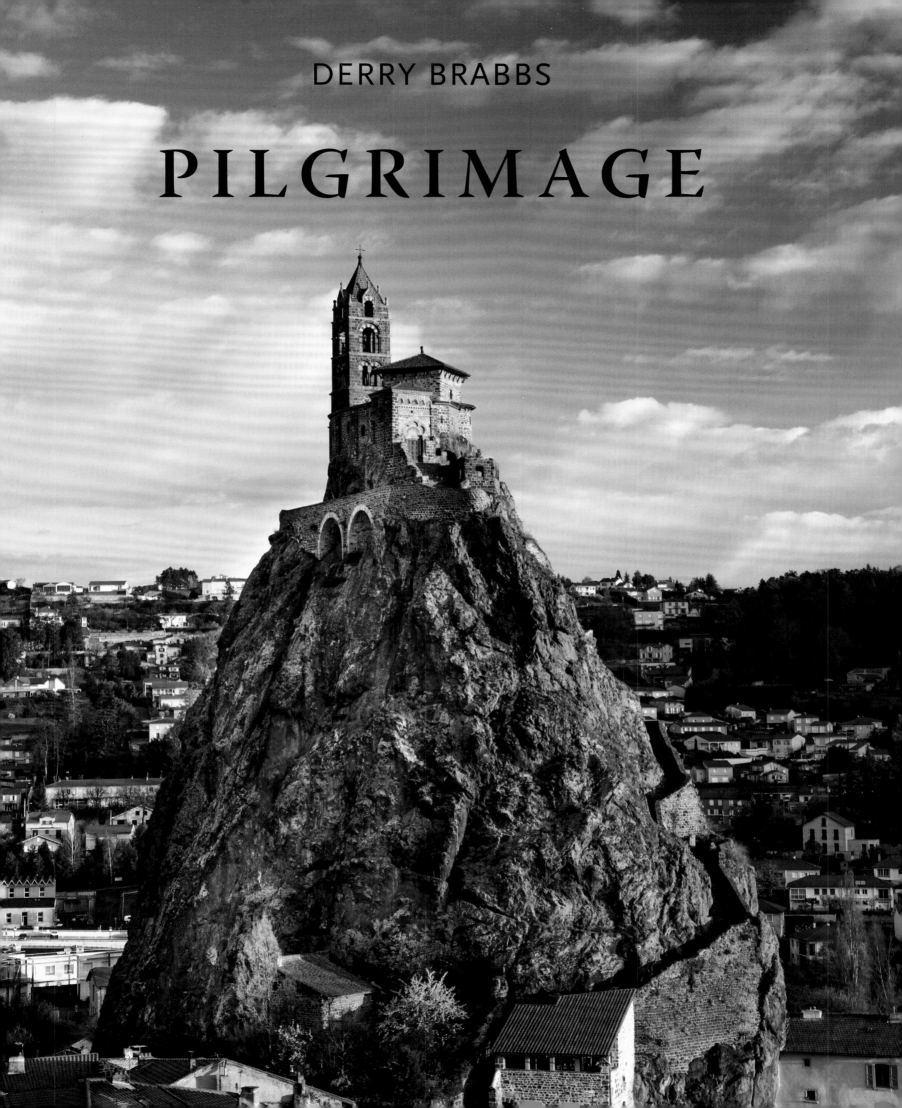

DERRY BRABBS

PILGRIMAGE

DERRY BRABBS

PILGRIMAGE

THE GREAT PILGRIM ROUTES OF BRITAIN AND EUROPE

FRANCES
LINCOLN

Pilgrimage

© 2017 Quarto Publishing plc

Text and photographs © Derry Brabbs 2017
Maps © Shutterstock
Designed by Arianna Osti

First Published in 2017 by Frances Lincoln,
an imprint of The Quarto Group.
The Old Brewery, 6 Blundell Street,
London N7 9BH, United Kingdom.
T (0)20 7700 6700 F (0)20 7700 8066
www.QuartoKnows.com

A catalogue record for this book is available from the British Library.

ISBN 978-0-7112-3900-5

Printed and bound in China

9 8 7 6 5 4

(Previous pages) The Calzada Romana is a long stretch of Roman road on the Camino Francés to the east of León. It was originally built to transport gold from the mines in Galicia back to Rome and also carried soldiers from both sides of the Muslim–Christian conflict during the early years of the Reconquest of Spain. *(This page)* The swirling mists of sunrise lingering over the surrounding plateau photographed from the high ramparts of Langres in the Champagne-Ardennes region. Seven gates and the same number of towers remain in their original places within the 2½ mile (3.5km) walls.

CONTENTS

INTRODUCTION

The rural roads, bridle tracks and footpaths of Europe are once again echoing with the sound of pilgrims' feet following a resurgence that began during the latter decades of the twentieth century.

That renewed interest can be largely attributed to the Council of Europe's initiative in creating a series of European Cultural Routes. The first to receive that accolade (in 1987) was the Camino Francés, the pilgrimage route across northern Spain from the Pyrenees to the shrine of St James the Apostle in Santiago de Compostela. Its historical and religious significance was further consolidated when the Camino was added to the UNESCO list of World Heritage Sites in 1993. The publicity and funding for the regeneration of existing infrastructure and the creation of new signage and pilgrim accommodation produced a gradual increase in numbers at first but this became a rapid escalation in the twenty-first century. Cathedral records show that the number of pilgrims recorded as having received the official *compostela* certificate rose from 3,500 in 1988 up to an extraordinary total of 277,000 in 2016. As a consequence of the vast numbers now walking the Camino Francés, many more are deterred by the daily scramble to secure available hostel bed spaces at the next overnight halt (usually free or at minimal cost to pilgrims carrying the *credencial* or pilgrim's passport). However, there are alternative routes in Spain and for those seeking to make their pilgrimage in a less stressful environment, there is no more appropriate challenge than the Vía de la Plata, a 460-mile (740km) route following the Roman road from Seville to join the main route in Astorga. And for those who seek to make a pilgrimage in the true spirit of their medieval counterparts and are willing to do it without the tangible reward of the *compostela,* there are other options to consider. The pilgrim routes to Santiago spread eastwards far beyond the four acknowledged starting points in France and there is actually such a comprehensive network within Germany that if one had the time, resources and stamina it would be possible to follow the Jakobsweg (Way of St James) all the way to Galicia from the shores of the Baltic. However, as an introduction to the wider possibilities available I have offered an insight into just two of the routes in Germany starting from Cologne and Munich. The other (very) long-distance European

The ancient Spanish walled city of Cáceres in Extremadura lies on the Vía de la Plata pilgrim route to Santiago de Compostela. The old town stands completely intact and aloof in the south-east corner of the modern conurbation. It is surprisingly compact with walls that are only about ¾ mile (1.1km) long and although the narrow streets and alleyways within that defensive perimeter do exude an aura of security, there is more than a hint of claustrophobia too. Some of the finest buildings are the dignified palaces built by the noble families that ruled here between the fourteenth and sixteenth centuries.

pilgrim route steadily increasing in popularity is the 1,180-mile (1,900km) Via Francigena from Canterbury to Rome. It too has benefited from Cultural Route status but although now clearly waymarked through both Switzerland and Italy, an officially designated pedestrian route through France has yet to be finalized. The French leg of the Via Francigena highlights the problem route planners have had to deal with in both France and elsewhere, namely that many of the principal Roman roads used by medieval travellers are now either motorways or major roads.

One obvious difference between journeys made in the twelfth century and today is that unlike their medieval counterparts, few of today's pilgrims will be retracing their steps and returning home on foot. Today's pilgrim will probably forego the ritual of a special mass at which the pilgrim's standard 'uniform' of cloak, wide-brimmed hat, wooden staff and bag is consecrated. A long journey overland in the Middle Ages was not something to be lightly undertaken and even if one were fit enough to cope with the rigours of travel, the risk of harm

from robbers was constant and very real. Preying upon bands of pilgrims evolved into a lucrative international business attracting organized gangs of villains who each marked out their own territory. Any person of substance about to embark on a pilgrimage also made his (seldom 'her') will, naming his heirs and the period of time which was to elapse before he should be presumed dead and the will executed.

I planned this book as a celebration of the legacy left by to us by the concept of pilgrimage and its manifestation in the glorious churches, cathedrals and sublime examples of craftsmanship in wood, stone and glass that brought them alive. I have combined well-known routes with less familiar ones from six European countries and I do hope that you share my pleasure in not only finding new landscapes and outstanding examples of Romanesque and Gothic architecture in some places that were hitherto unfamiliar, but also enjoy becoming reacquainted with familiar favourites on the more well trodden routes. And I hope that you are inspired to set out on a long and purposeful walk.

Lucca, Tuscany. The church of San Michele in Foro was built on the site of the Roman forum and is a sublime example of the Pisan Romanesque architectural style. Its richly decorated high façade comprises four arcades whose rows of marble Corinthian columns are worked in contrasting styles.

ROUTES

ST CUTHBERT'S WAY

Melrose Abbey · Morebattle · Wooler · Holy Island
St Boswells · Wideopen Hill · St Cuthbert's Cave

THE PILGRIMS WAY

Winchester · Guildford · Canterbury
Farnham · St Martha's Hill · Maidstone · Dover

LES CHEMINS DU MONT-SAINT-MICHEL

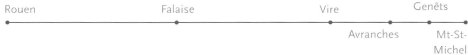

Rouen · Falaise · Vire · Genêts
Avranches · Mt-St-Michel

VIA PODIENSIS & CAMINO FRANCÉS

Le Puy-en-Velay · Figeac · Moissac · Ostabat-Asme
Conques · Cahors · Estella
León · Estella
Santiago de Compostela · Burgos · Logroño · St-Jean-Pied-de-Port

VÍA DE LA PLATA

Seville · Zafra · Salamanca · Astorga
Mérida · Cáceres · Zamora

VIA COLONIENSIS

Cologne · Blankenheim · Waxweiler
Bad Münstereifel · Prüm · Trier

MÜNCHNER JAKOBSWEG

Munich · Wessobrunn · Kempten
Andechs · Steingaden · Lindau

VIA DI FRANCESCO

La Verna · Gubbio
Città di Castello · Assisi

VIA FRANCIGENA

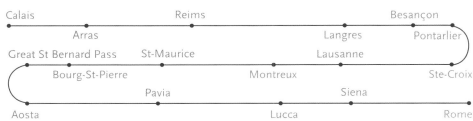

Calais · Reims · Besançon
Arras · Langres · Pontarlier
Great St Bernard Pass · St-Maurice · Lausanne
Bourg-St-Pierre · Montreux · Ste-Croix
Pavia · Siena
Aosta · Lucca · Rome

ST CUTHBERT'S WAY

Melrose Abbey to Holy Island

62 MILES / 5 DAYS

St Cuthbert's Way is not a historic route of pilgrimage in the generally acknowledged sense, as it only opened in 1996. The route's starting point at Melrose in the Scottish Borders was where Cuthbert spent his formative years as a monk, and its final destination on Lindisfarne (Holy Island) is where the saint was buried after his death in 687. Cleverly combining leisurely sections alongside the mighty River Tweed with quite strenuous climbs over the foothills of the Cheviots, St Cuthbert's Way can easily be accomplished in five days. The prevailing winds in the United Kingdom blow in from the Atlantic, so any cross-country walks are best done from west to east with the worst of the weather on one's back. Happily, the suggested route tracing the natural progression of St Cuthbert's life runs that way, although some walkers do still prefer to start their journey from the iconic island of Lindisfarne.

St Cuthbert's Way was partly established to create economic benefits for communities along the way, especially as significant portions of the route pass through sparsely populated areas of the Borders region. Individual households, hamlets and villages located on pilgrim routes worldwide have long derived much-needed additional income by providing food and lodging for the pilgrims who in essence were the first tourists. Although primarily designed as a long distance walk between two St Cuthbert-related points, it has rapidly acquired the status of a pilgrimage and been readily adopted as such by Christian groups and individuals alike.

St Cuthbert's Way was an inspired choice but to bring it to fruition in just eighteen months required a huge amount of cross-border cooperation between English and Scottish official bodies and the landowners whose consent was needed to route the path where no Public Rights of Way existed. These bureaucratic processes can drag on interminably but the speed with which permissions were granted and route-marking completed is an indication of just how much St Cuthbert still means to his native region.

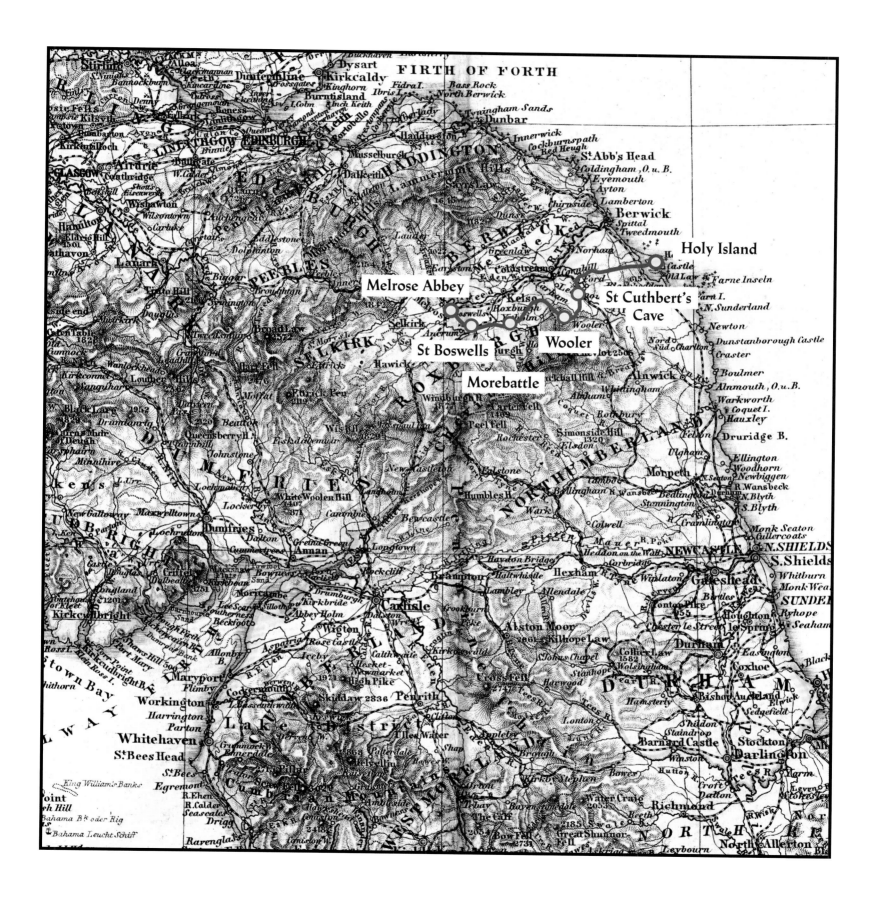

It would be difficult to find a more evocative starting point for a pilgrimage than the substantial pale red sandstone remains of Melrose Abbey *(opposite)*. The early Christian community Cuthbert joined as a teenager and subsequently rose to become its prior was actually located at Old Melrose (known then as *Maelros*), an isolated and now deserted site on privately owned land some 2 miles (3km) downstream on the River Tweed. It was established around AD 635 at the behest of Oswald, King of Northumbria, who desired that his kingdom should follow his own recent conversion to Christianity. It was amid that period of early missionary zeal that Cuthbert flourished at *Maelros* and he was regarded as one of the most influential figures in the early Celtic Christian Church.

The Cistercian abbey of Melrose was founded in 1136 but, in common with the other great Border abbeys established by King David I of Scotland, it was subjected to attacks during the many cross-border conflicts that ebbed and flowed between England and Scotland during the later Middle Ages. The abbey suffered serious damage by English forces under Edward I in 1300 and 1307 and by Edward II in 1322 but it was the assault by Richard II in 1385 that all but destroyed the place and the abbey had to be completely rebuilt.

It is difficult to equate such a flamboyant architectural essay in the late Decorated and early Perpendicular styles of Gothic architecture with the customary Cistercian austerity but by the time reconstruction got under way, a more relaxed approach to monastic life had permeated through many orders and so the finest stonemasons and craftsmen were employed to create a new abbey church with extravagant detail and complex tracery in the windows. Melrose eventually succumbed to the same fate as all monastic foundations in the sixteenth century as Scotland severed ties with the Roman Catholic church but, in common with many other abbeys that also served local communities, three bays of the nave were retained for use as the parish church, a role it maintained until the early nineteenth century, when a new place of worship in the town was commissioned.

Although there will probably never be conclusive proof, it is likely that the casket discovered during early-twentieth-century archaeological excavations contains the embalmed heart of the legendary Scottish king, Robert the Bruce (1274–1329), the rest of whose body is interred at Dunfermline Abbey.

Wideopen Hill is the highest point on St Cuthbert's Way and is also roughly the halfway point of the walk. Seldom has a landscape feature been so aptly named because with every step of the ascent the views in all direction towards the Cheviots and the twin communities of Kirk and Town Yetholm are spectacular, belying the summit's height of just 1,207ft (368m). The distinctive signposts bearing St Cuthbert's Cross show the line of the route in both directions and the path in between the waymarkers is becoming well trodden and easy to follow, even in conditions of poor visibility.

(Right) The overhanging sandstone outcrop of St Cuthbert's Cave is an atmospheric place that truly evokes the spirit of the pilgrimage. *(Overleaf)* The causeway from the mainland to Lindisfarne at sunrise. The raised wooden hut is a place of refuge for anyone foolishly caught out by the rapid incoming tide.

Following its first (and highest) excursion over the northern flanks of the Cheviots, the route of St Cuthbert's Way offers temporary respite for walkers as it descends from the summit of Wideopen Hill towards the village of Town Yetholm. Lying just a short distance across the valley of the fast flowing Bowmont Water is the smaller community of Kirk Yetholm, whose name is synonymous with the 268-mile (431km) Pennine Way that runs from Edale in Derbyshire's Peak District up the Pennine backbone of England to its conclusion just over the Scottish Border at Kirk Yetholm. Pilgrims will probably encounter limping and bedraggled Pennine Way walkers heading towards them on the road leading out of Kirk Yetholm but shortly thereafter the St Cuthbert's Way path charts its own course towards the border fence between England and Scotland and the start of a truly exhilarating section of the route across some of Northumberland's finest countryside.

Dramatic landscapes are not the only feature of the middle sectors of St Cuthbert's Way: as the route approaches Wooler, the distinctive twin-humped summit of Yeavering Bell fills the skyline ahead. This is this one of the region's most impressive Iron Age hill forts and in its shadow lies Ed Gefrin, one of the most remarkable archaeological finds of the twentieth century. Ed Gefrin was the vast seventh-century royal palace of King Edwin of Northumbria. Subsequent excavations revealed a complex of great halls, some of which exceeded 80ft (25m) in length and also what appears to have been some kind of theatre with stepped seating.

Although perhaps less spectacular in the wider historical context, St Cuthbert's Cave is of paramount importance to pilgrims bound for Holy Island. The persistent Viking raids during the ninth century that had made life on the island virtually untenable for the monks of Lindisfarne came to a head in 875 when they were finally forced to retreat onto the mainland. They carried the coffin containing St Cuthbert's perfectly preserved corpse with them and according to legend (where would we be without them?) this complex of sandstone caves is where they rested on that first night. The community of Lindisfarne spent many decades thereafter seeking sanctuary, solitude and peace with their precious cargo and it was not until 995 that they finally settled in Durham, whose majestic cathedral still houses the relics and coffin of St Cuthbert.

There are two routes by which pilgrims and visitors can access Lindisfarne from the mainland but whether making the traditional crossing over the sands or using the tarmac causeway, both can only be attempted at low tide. The traditional crossing is marked by a long line of tall marker posts set into the sand but even with that clearly marked route it is still not advisable to attempt it unless accompanied by someone with local knowledge.

Few places exhibit the spirit of early Christianity as much as Lindisfarne and one somehow becomes enveloped in the timeless atmosphere that pervades the island. The first monastery established here in AD 635 by St Aidan probably followed the Irish tradition of simple huts grouped around a basic timber church that would have borne no resemblance to the later medieval foundation. The ruins of that solid Romanesque priory church *(opposite, above)* are famous for the 'rainbow arch', a single surviving vault rib from the crossing and it is extraordinary how one fragment of stone can be so symbolic, signifying for many the enduring strength of Christianity.

St Cuthbert was a significant contributor to the spread of Christianity during the seventh century but his missionary zeal was interspersed with periods of solitude and reflection. He withdrew to a small island adjacent to Lindisfarne but actually preferred the even greater isolation of the Farne Islands further out into the North Sea and it was there that he died in AD 687. He was buried beneath the church on Lindisfarne but when disinterred for enshrinement over a decade later, the monks discovered his corpse exhibited no signs of decomposition. Cuthbert's body was reverentially installed in a new wooden coffin that remained unburied next to the altar.

This miraculous event was probably the inspiration behind one of Celtic Christianity's greatest treasures, the Lindisfarne Gospels, a work instigated by Bishop Eadfrith around AD 700. Its 258 pages are beautifully inscribed and decorated throughout but the book's crowning glory is the introductory page to each gospel, featuring intricate lettering and colour of indescribable intensity. This artistic masterpiece is now housed in the British Museum.

St Cuthbert's Way starts and finishes amid the imposing ruins of two important medieval monastic communities and for anyone walking the route as an act of pilgrimage, the section over the Cheviot foothills *(opposite, below left and right)* that crosses from Scotland into England provides ample opportunity for solitude and reflection.

ST WINEFRIDE'S WELL

Holywell

S t Winefride's Well is set on a steep hillside below the north Welsh town of Holywell. It has been a place of pilgrimage for over 1,300 years and the vast numbers of documented miracle cures have resulted in it being christened the 'Lourdes of Wales'. However, when the winds howl in from the Dee estuary, it can feel rather more like Siberia than the south of France. The origins of the seventh-century well and the young woman after whom it was named are an intriguing combination of fact and fantasy.

Winefride (Gwenfrewi in Welsh) was a nun destined for life in a convent and whose spiritual tutor was a monk named Beuno. The villain of the legend is Caradoc, a local prince who took exception to his amorous advances being rejected by Winefride and in a drunken rage cut off her head with a single blow from his sword. On the spot where the saint's head landed, a spring of water gushed from the earth and later this was discovered to be endowed with miraculous healing properties. At the time of the incident Beuno was praying in his church nearby and upon hearing the commotion ran over and managed to successfully reunite Winefride's severed head with her body. Her attacker was 'swallowed up into the ground' although it is more likely that he was killed in an act of revenge by Winefride's brother, Owain. Winefride did eventually became abbess of the convent at Gwytherin and when she died there her grave attracted many pilgrims. Her fame and that of the well spread and Holywell became an important place of pilgrimage with contemporary chroniclers recording visits by king Richard I the Lionheart in 1189, Henry V in 1416 upon his safe return from victory at Agincourt. In 1686, James II and his wife, Mary of Modena came to Holywell to seek St Winefride's help in conceiving a male heir. Although cynics might suggest it was a 50/50 chance, their son James Francis Edward (the 'Old Pretender') was born in June 1688.

(Opposite) The chapel encasing St Winefride's Well was built in the sixteenth century to replace an earlier church on the site. One of its benefactors was thought to be Henry VII's mother, Lady Margaret, Countess of Richmond, whose coat of arms is one of several emblazoned on the roof bosses.

(Previous pages, left) A stained-glass window in the upper floor chapel depicts the martyrdom of St Winefride. (Previous pages, right) The spring emerges into a star-shaped basin surrounded by an ambulatory. The pillars support a vaulted ceiling adorned with roof bosses in a magnificent example of Perpendicular Gothic architecture.

(Opposite) The niche statue of St Winefride dates from the late-ninteenth century, replacing the original that was destroyed during the Reformation. (Left) Maen Achwyfan is a remarkable early Christian wheel cross standing near Holywell. It was fashioned from one large slab of stone and stands 11ft (3.4m) high.

THE PILGRIMS WAY

Winchester to Dover

132 MILES / 11 DAYS

The Pilgrims Way linked the cathedral shrines of St Swithun in Winchester and Thomas Becket in Canterbury. However, their status as two of the most important places of pilgrimage in medieval Britain was severely diminished when those glorious, jewel-encrusted shrines joined the nation's other religious iconography on the post-Reformation bonfire, albeit minus their precious gemstones. Pilgrims would not necessarily have followed one particular designated route in the way that walkers are now shepherded along clearly marked footpaths, but would have used the existing tracks that had served travellers and tradesmen since prehistoric times. These ancient routes used by Neolithic settlers that ran just below the ridge of the chalk downs formed an important trade route between the eastern Channel ports and England's West Country. Some variants did veer south from Farnham towards Winchester but the main 'highway' continued westwards towards Salisbury Plain, Stonehenge and from the Bronze Age onwards, down to the tin mines of Cornwall.

The Pilgrims Way of today is actually an amalgamation of two separate walking trails – the 34-mile (55km) St Swithun's Way from Winchester to Farnham and the North Downs Way National Trail, opened in 1978, that begins in Farnham and follows the line of the Downs through Surrey and Kent to the English Channel at Dover but with an optional Canterbury loop included.

Close scrutiny of the relevant Ordnance Survey maps shows how the North Downs Way is either incorporated into, or runs almost parallel to, the old footpaths which are marked as either *Pilgrims Way* or simply *Trackway*. The Pilgrims Way almost certainly acquired its title from Victorian cartographers who perhaps sought to add a sense of romanticism to such an historic route. Two eminent writers of that period, Julia Cartwright Ady (1851–1924) and Hilaire Belloc (1870–1953) both wrote narrative guidebooks although only the former used the name 'Pilgrims Way' whereas Belloc simply referred to it as the 'Old Road'. Although twenty-first-century pilgrims follow an amended route in order to avoid major roads, there are enough surviving segments of the original to engender a sense of empathy with their medieval counterparts.

Winchester is one of the longest and most impressive Gothic cathedrals in Western Europe, an assertion one would initially dispute based on its plain, unadorned exterior. However, as soon as you enter the soaring, fourteenth-century Perpendicular nave, any such doubts are dispelled and, when viewed from the main west front portal, the church appears even longer than its actual length of 558ft (170m). Work on the present church began in 1079 under the direction of Walkelin, a Norman bishop appointed by William the Conqueror, and Romanesque architecture from that period survives in both transepts and the crypt. The new building replaced the Old Minster, the Saxon cathedral that housed the shrine of St Swithun, the ninth-century Bishop of Winchester whose name will be forever associated with wet English summers. According to legend, if it rains during the saint's feast day on 15 July, similar weather will endure for another forty days thereafter and if the sun shines then the same rule applies.

St Swithun's shrine was moved from the Old Minster into the Norman cathedral but as word of the healing miracles attributed to the saint spread further afield, pilgrim numbers increased to such an extent that the retrochoir was built during the thirteenth century to allow even greater access to the shrine. The small memorial replica in the retrochoir *(opposite, above left)* stands on the same floor of medieval encaustic tiles *(opposite, above right)* upon which St Swithun's lavishly gilded shrine stood until destroyed by Henry VIII's commissioners in 1538. A basic red Wessex clay tile was imprinted with a wooden stamp while the clay was still malleable and the resulting mould then filled with a contrasting white clay, after which the combination was glazed and fired.

Winchester is renowned for its collection of seven chantry chapels, more than any other English cathedral and a reflection of the status, wealth and power of both the church and the bishops who built them. These miniature masterpieces of ecclesiastical architecture span a period of almost 200 years beginning with William of Edington in 1346 through to Stephen Gardiner in the mid-sixteenth century. Standing immediately to the north of St Swithun's shrine is the chantry chapel of William Wayneflete *(opposite, below)*, Bishop of Winchester from 1447–86. Prior to his appointment as bishop he had been the first headmaster of Eton College. He also founded Oxford's Magdalen College in 1458.

(Below) The massive twelfth-century carved font originated
in Tournai, Belgium and was gifted to the cathedral by
Henry of Blois, Bishop of Winchester from 1129–71.
Although referred to as the black 'Tournai marble' font, it
is actually polished limestone. The finely detailed graphic
carvings adorning each side depict scenes from the life of
St Nicholas. *(Opposite)* The elegant fourteenth-century wood
screen dividing the nave and choir is so delicately carved
that it perfectly complements the soaring stonework of the
nave. The twelfth-century tomb in the foreground is thought
to be that of Bishop Henry of Blois.

As its name implies, the church of St Martha-on-the-Hill occupies an elevated position on the Pilgrims Way and is certainly one of the route's highlights. There are claims that up to eight English counties can be seen on a clear day, but as the site is heavily wooded on all but the south-facing side, pilgrims will probably be more than content to simply enjoy the view from this bench with its own sandy beach. The added joy of this place is that it is normally accessible only on foot and so its aura of tranquillity is not disrupted by the intrusive sound of motor vehicles. There is a long history of Christian worship on this site dating back to a Saxon church listed in the Domesday Book. A Norman church replaced that building and from the thirteenth century, it was occupied and enlarged by Augustinian canons. The present church was reconstructed during the mid-nineteenth century from the ruins of its predecessor that had been virtually destroyed in 1745 by a devastating accidental blast from an explosives factory in the Tillingbourne Valley below. The mills and factories that once filled the surrounding landscape have long since disappeared, leaving St Martha-on-the-Hill once more in peaceful isolation.

(Left) Newlands Corner is a popular beauty spot near Guildford offering spectacular views over the Surrey Hills. It was near here in 1926 that the crime writer Agatha Christie mysteriously disappeared but was discovered eleven days later staying under a pseudonym at a hotel in Harrogate, North Yorkshire. *(Below)* Jane Austen's house in Chawton near Alton is now a museum dedicated to her life and work. She spent the last eight years of her life here from 1809–17. *(Bottom)* Farnham Castle was built by Bishop Henry de Blois in 1138 and became the residence for subsequent bishops of Winchester.

Chalk landscape on the North Downs Way at Detling near Maidstone. The word 'downs' seems strange when applied to an area of hills and ridges but is actually derived from the Old English *dun*, meaning 'hill'. The chalk of the downs was formed from the skeletons of billions of marine creatures deposited during the Upper Cretaceous period some 85 million years ago when the area was still covered by sea. Tectonic plate movements caused the formation of the ridges of what are now the North and South Downs and the gradual erosion of the softer rocks on the south side of the North Downs formed the steep slope, or 'scarp'. This whole region was once covered in dense woodland, the clearance of which for agriculture began back in the Neolithic period. The open landscape created by those early farmers was subsequently maintained by extensive sheep grazing but when that practice died out in the late-nineteenth century, the classic wildflower-rich grassland of the open downs was lost to scrub and woodland. Arable farming and urban sprawl are further eating into this traditional landscape but thankfully vast tracts of this unique landscape are now protected by law against further intrusive development.

Canterbury Cathedral's 250ft (76m) central tower dominates the medieval core of the city originally named Durovernum by the Romans. It was at Canterbury in AD 597 that St Augustine began his crusade at the behest of Pope Gregory to bring Christianity back to England and his first cathedral thereby made Canterbury the cradle of English Christianity and subsequently Mother Church of the Anglican faith. The cathedral was all but destroyed by fire in 1067, just one year after the Norman Conquest. William I installed Lanfranc as archbishop to restore the cathedral although his work was all but obliterated by another serious fire in 1174, an event that could have had dire consequences for Canterbury's future.

Just four year earlier in 1170, the then Archbishop of Canterbury, Thomas Becket was murdered in his cathedral by four of Henry II's knights in response to their kings exasperated, but probably, rhetorical question 'Will no one rid me of this turbulent priest?' Becket's martyrdom, canonization just three years later and his subsequent enshrinement led to Canterbury becoming the greatest pilgrimage destination in the country. Had it not been for the fact that Becket's tomb was lodged down in the magnificent crypt built by Lanfranc, the means by which Canterbury Cathedral could secure its future could have literally gone up in smoke.

Reconstruction of the cathedral's interior was undertaken during two phases of development separated by 200 years. The Trinity Chapel was designed to host the saint's shrine and it was stroke of architectural genius to elevate each section of the church as it progressed eastwards. Flights of stone steps ran upwards on either side of the nave and then up again to the choir to create a sensation of triumphant ascension towards the high altar and the glittering, jewel encrusted shrine beyond. The steady flow of income from pilgrims and the gifts and endowments from wealthy nobles anxious to secure the best possible afterlife ensured that further work was possible and by the last quarter of the fourteenth century, Lanfranc's nave had been rebuilt and by 1500, the tower had been added and that is the cathedral we see today. The main entrance into the cathedral precincts is *via* the Christ Church Gate *(opposite)*, begun in 1501 by Henry VII to honour his eldest son, Prince Arthur and his bride, Catherine of Aragon.

(Overleaf) Canterbury Cathedral seen across the seemingly diminutive rooftops of the old city. This view makes one realize just how powerful and awe-inspiring the Church and its alternating messages of hope and doom must have appeared to ordinary people in the Middle Ages.

The Via Francigena (see page 184) begins its long and
arduous journey to Rome from Canterbury Cathedral and a
marker stone bearing the route's distinctive logo *(right)* is set
immediately next to the main portal. *(Above)* St Augustine's
abbey lies just outside Canterbury's city walls on the route
of the Via Francigena. The ruins of the medieval monastery
occupy the site of Augustine's first church, founded in 597
and are now in the care of English heritage. *(Opposite)*
The White Cliffs of Dover tinged with pink from the first
flush of sunrise and from where the journey to Rome starts
in earnest.

LES CHEMINS DU MONT-SAINT-MICHEL

Rouen to Mont-Saint-Michel

205 MILES / 15 DAYS

After many years of being attached to the mainland *via* a solid raised causeway that resulted in severe silting up of the surrounding bay, the iconic island of Mont-Saint-Michel has once again been set free by the construction of a road bridge on stilts. The bay is now well on its way to becoming fully restored back to nature and the rocky island once again surrounded by water at high tide. The new access road is just one element in the campaign to efficiently and sympathetically manage the mass tourism that will forever be part of the everyday life of Mont-Saint-Michel. Fortunately, the tradition of pilgrimage is still very much alive and even more so now that the routes to Mont-Saint-Michel once trodden by medieval pilgrims were collectively adopted as a Cultural Route of the Council of Europe in 2007. Veneration of St Michael the Archangel can be traced back to the earliest periods of Christianity and in addition to the countless churches named in his honour, he also provided a rich source of inspiration in art. He was graphically portrayed as both a sword-wielding heavenly hero and also as the angel holding the scales upon which the souls of the dead are weighed at the Last Judgment, a sculpted tableau that regularly features on the tympana of pilgrimage abbeys and churches. The medieval cult of St Michael was popular in Britain and many pilgrims sailed from English ports to visit Mont-Saint-Michel before continuing south towards Santiago de Compostela. However, two of the most travelled routes in the Middle Ages were from Rouen and Caen, the former being an important conduit over the River Seine for those *en route* from Picardy and the Low Countries. After extensive footpath restoration and signposting, the organization bearing the same title as these routes, Les Chemins du Mont-Saint-Michel, have recreated those two long distance pilgrimage trails. The Rouen option is 205 miles (330km) and from Caen, the journey is 99 miles (160km). The two routes converge on the bay's eastern shoreline at Genêts for the final trek across the salt marshes and sands to the abbey.

The west front of Rouen Cathedral *(opposite)* was the glorious sight that greeted the great Impressionist painter Claude Monet every day from the makeshift studios he set up opposite the cathedral in 1892 and again the following year. Although Monet was renowned for his groups of paintings exploring the effects of light on a single subject, the Rouen series was his most prolific from one site. He returned to Paris with thirty canvases that were reworked during 1894 and then edited down to a final selection of twenty. The cathedral of Notre-Dame is France's tallest cathedral and for just four years in the 1880s was the world record holder until eclipsed by Cologne Cathedral. However, those extra metres were actually the result of a nineteenth-century cast-iron spire built on top of the lantern tower. A decades-long restoration programme conducted behind swathes of photographer-unfriendly tarpaulin has revealed the stonework in its true light and all the sculptures on the art gallery that is the west front are outstanding. The central portal is dedicated to the Virgin with an elaborate Tree of Jesse in the tympanum, the left-hand one is St John the Baptist and right-hand portal is dedicated to St Stephen, the first Christian martyr.

The main street leading directly away from the cathedral passes through the medieval quarter and a glorious *mélange* of colourful half-timbered houses, many of which had to be rebuilt after war damage. Having passed under the arch bearing the Grand Horloge, one approaches the Place du Vieux Marché (old market square), the spot where Joan of Arc was burnt at the stake by the English in 1431. Rouen was just one of many parts of France then ruled by the English but, as the Hundred Years War entered its final two decades after the martyrdom of Joan of Arc, the tides of fortune swung towards the French and when victory was secured in 1453, only Calais remained in English hands. Most of the French kings up to the sixteenth century would have made the pilgrimage from Rouen to Mont-Saint-Michel and this long route is definitely one for those seeking the tranquillity of nature because long stretches are either through typical French forests or vast tracts of open countryside. Few pilgrimages can have such a spectacular denouement as the first sighting of Mont-Saint-Michel's Benedictine abbey perched on its rugged little offshore island.

(Above) The heart of Rouen's half-timbered medieval quarter has been so perfectly restored it is like being transported back through the centuries in a time machine but without the underfoot hazards of fifteenth-century street life.

(Right) A statue to the French heroine Joan of Arc stands in a side chapel of the cathedral, just a short distance away from the square where she was burnt at the stake in 1431.

(Opposite) The architectural ensemble of Rouen's Gros Horloge comprises a Gothic belfry, a Renaissance archway and clock face behind which is fully functioning fourteenth-century mechanism.

Towns and villages with even the most tenuous links to the Dukes of Normandy will claim closer ties with William the Conqueror than the reality of history would confirm. However, Falaise is one place with impeccable credentials in that respect because it was here that the future King William I of England was born in 1027. The magnificent bronze equestrian statue to *Guillaume le Conquérant (opposite)* is set on a large stone plinth bearing smaller statues of six previous Dukes of Normandy, beginning with the earliest and most unlikely sounding candidate, Rollo the Viking. Rollo and his Scandinavian raiders had originally sailed up the River Seine to Rouen from where they launched campaigns of mayhem and destruction over a wide area. In an attempt to stabilize the situation, Charles III (the tenth-century Carolingian King of France) offered to give Rollo vast swathes of Northern France in return for peace and the Viking's conversion to Christianity. As a result of the deal in 911 the dynasty of the Dukes of Normandy was therefore founded on the genes of a Viking warrior. The sixth statue on the plinth is of Robert the Magnificent who held the title from 1027–35 and was the father of William the Conqueror, albeit by his mistress Herleva, a local tanner's daughter. William inherited the title at the tender age of seven when his father died on a pilgrimage to Jerusalem and, until lauded with the sobriquet 'Conqueror' decades later, he was more commonly referred to as William the Bastard. The statue was erected in 1851 between the Gothic church of La Trinité and the gateway to the vast castle of the Dukes of Normandy. The French word *falaise* means 'cliff' and the craggy hill above the River Ante upon which the original castle was established could not have been better chosen. The dour fortress and donjon visitors see today was built during the twelfth and thirteenth centuries to replace the earlier castle of the Dukes of Normandy in which William had been born. Work on the new castle was begun in 1123 by the Conqueror's fourth son who at that time was ruling as both King Henry I of England and also Duke of Normandy, having wrested power from his elder brother Robert. Falaise was a casualty of the post-D-Day fighting in Normandy but has restored its churches and historic buildings to replicate the originals.

Although Falaise was the birthplace of William the Conqueror, Caen – the starting point of another of the Chemins du Mont-Saint-Michel – was where he built his own mighty fortress. The other significant buildings from that period are two abbeys founded by William and his wife, Matilda of Flanders, the Abbaye aux Hommes and the Abbaye aux Dames respectively. Both monastic foundations were established as an act of penance for ignoring a papal ban on their marriage by Leo IX in 1049 on the grounds of consanguinity. William and Matilda were actually third cousins once removed and consequently in breach of the strict guidelines that demanded a minimum gap of seven generations or degrees of relatedness and so the abbeys were offered as a means of ending their excommunication and hopefully smoothing the path through into the next life. The church of La Trinité *(opposite, above left)* was built using the locally quarried pale Caen limestone, a building material so sought after that once William was crowned king of England on Christmas Day 1066, he began shipping it across the English Channel to be used in places such as Canterbury Cathedral and the Tower of London. La Trinité originally had twin spires but these were torn down from the towers during the Hundred Years War and replaced by balustrades in the early 1700s. The tympanum over the main entrance portal *(opposite, below right)* is a late-nineteenth-century homage to the original and comprises the Holy Trinity in human form plus symbolic representations of the four Evangelists. The Caen stone is seen to particularly good effect in the church's very plain but atmospheric interior adorned by pure Romanesque round arches and decorated capitals. The apse *(opposite, above right)* has benefited aesthetically from the late-twentieth-century restoration in which the subtle low level directional lighting creates sublime textures upon the carefully worked stone. In the ceiling dome is an early-eighteenth-century painting of the Assumption of the Virgin Mary and in a corner of the nave, a small collection of church vestments *(opposite, below left)* exhibits the same high level of craftsmanship and creative skill employed throughout the building. La Trinité was founded in 1059 and work began three years later to be finally completed in 1130. The body of Queen Matilda was interred in the church beneath a large slab of black Tournai marble following her death in 1083, four years before her husband, William the Conqueror.

(Overleaf, left) The basilica of Saint-Gervais, Avranches, is renowned for its collection of religious treasures and in the context of the pilgrimage, none could be more significant than the much revered skull of St Aubert, the eighth-century Bishop of Avrances, who is attributed with founding the first religious community on Mont-Saint-Michel. *(Right)* Vire. The twelfth-century Saint-Thomas was Vire's oldest church but in common with most of the town, did not survive the Allied bombing of 1944. The surviving ivy-clad entrance portal and lower part of the bell tower now stand alone as a poignant reminder of past times.

According to the legend regarding the foundation of Mont-Saint-Michel, it took three appearances by the archangel in the dreams of Bishop Aubert of Avranches to persuade him to build a sanctuary on the deserted granite island then known as Mont Tombe. The fortunes of the small religious community living on the island improved significantly when the importance of the shrine was acknowledged by the new rulers of Normandy and the 3rd Duke, Richard I installed Benedictine monks there in 966. Gifts from pilgrims and rich endowments enabled further expansion and both the monastic and church buildings began their centuries long struggle against the elements, lack of space and gravity. It does not matter what time of day you view the island because its glorious conglomeration of cleverly tiered stone perched on a huge high rock will always present a dream-like appearance and few other sites so perfectly manifest the absolute power of faith in the context of medieval Christianity. The pilgrimage routes from Rouen and Caen employ a distinctive logo *(opposite, above left)* combining Mont-Saint-Michel with the now-universal symbol of pilgrimage – the scallop shell. The official footpath skirts around the bay to join up with the causeway but the grassy non-tidal foreshore of the bay *(opposite, above right)* is dotted with footpaths and if you do wander away from the signposted route it has to be with maximum caution. For anyone arriving in Genêts at the end of their pilgrimage and who seeks the unforgettable experience of the direct route, it can only be accomplished with a local guide who has experience of the tides and can negotiate a safe passage across the mudflats and quicksands. Throughout much of its existence, the abbey has been a fortress *(opposite, below left)* against both the sea and a succession of human assailants, most notably during the Hundred Years War when it survived numerous attacks and a maritime siege by English forces. The abbey church has suffered several structural disasters, not least when the entire choir collapsed without warning in 1421. It was later rebuilt in the Gothic Flamboyant style *(opposite, below right)* to create an interesting architectural juxtaposition between the choir's light and airy space and the severity and darkness of the earlier Romanesque nave. To fully savour the magic of Mont-Saint-Michel and avoid the worst of the crowds, you have to visit either out of season, midweek or early in the morning.

VIA PODIENSIS

Le Puy-en-Velay to St-Jean-Pied-de-Port

460 MILES / 30 DAYS

L e Puy-en-Velay was the starting point of the oldest recorded pilgrimage from France to Santiago de Compostela, made during the winter of AD 950–1 by Bishop Godescalc. Although we have *bona fide* documentary evidence of similar long distance journeys made during that period such as Archbishop Sigeric's between Canterbury and Rome, there were probably countless apocryphal accounts of pilgrimages made on the basis of wishful thinking rather than enduring the harsh reality of travel in the Middle Ages. Le Puy-en-Velay is a truly remarkable place set amid the remains of a volcanic landscape surrounded by bleak plateaux, rocky outcrops and soaring basalt pillars, three of which play a dominant role in the character of Le Puy. When viewed from a distance, the most dominant pinnacle appears to be the Corneille Rock, an impression amplified by the giant, garish orange statue of Notre-Dame-de-France erected on the summit. This extraordinary sculpture was fashioned from 213 melted down Russian cannons recovered by the French in 1855 after the Siege of Sebastopol during the Crimean War. A far smaller but infinitely more significant statue was the Black Virgin brought back from Palestine during the Crusades in 1254 by Louis IX and which instantly transformed the fortunes of the town when it became an important pilgrimage destination. As with most pilgrim routes throughout Europe, the Via Podiensis declined after the Reformation and even though Catholicism was again the dominant religion in France from the end of the sixteenth century, any revival in the tradition of pilgrimage was halted by the post Revolution secularization of France at the beginning of the ninteenth century. The wheel has now turned full circle and the steep flight of steps leading down from Le Puy's majestic cathedral are once again crowded with pilgrims taking their first steps on the 460 miles (740km) journey to the Pyrenees. The Via Podiensis has become the most popular of the four French options, combining an impressive number of historic sites such as Conques, Figeac, Cahors and Moissac interspersed with a varied and sometimes challenging set of different landscapes.

(Overleaf) The tiny Romanesque chapel of Saint-Michel d'Aiguilhe (the needle) is perched on the summit of a 280ft (85m) high volcanic rock that can be accessed only by means of 268 steps cut into the rock face. The chapel was built by Bishop Godescalc in celebration of his safe return from Santiago de Compostela and although a small sanctuary was first consecrated in 969, it was later enlarged into the predominately twelfth-century building extant today. The Islamic influences in the colour and design of the cathedral of Notre-Dame's stonework (see page 64, below) are even more pronounced on the chapel's main façade.

Le Puy-en-Velay
Rocamadour
Figeac
Cahors
Conques
Moissac
Ostabat-Asme
St-Jean-Pied-de-Port

Le-Puy-en-Velay has been renowned for its delicate lacemaking for over five centuries but is probably more famous for the small, green lentils unique to the region that flourish on the fertile volcanic soil. The fact that the town was built on an uneven bed of virtually impenetrable hard rock is evident from the topography of the cathedral of Notre-Dame. Regardless of whether you approach the cathedral from the small plateau at the foot of the Corneille Rock on which it stands or direct from the town centre, a steep climb is required. Only by making the direct approach do you get a true sense of just how complex the building process must have been and the resourcefulness required by the eleventh- and twelfth-century architects and masons who built it. When viewed from the foot of the steps, the west façade of Notre-Dame is an unforgettable sight; a vast tableau comprising five levels of polychrome masonry pierced by Romanesque style windows, arches and blind arcading. The ascent does not end at the main entrance portal because the staircase continues upwards before emerging into the final two bays of the nave that were added towards the end of the twelfth century and built on piles with massive arcading to compensate for the steepness of the slope. The first of the cathedral's two iconic statues to become visible is the Black Virgin on the high altar. Sadly this is just a copy of the original that was publicly burned by French Revolutionaries in 1794. An early-fifteenth-century wooden statue of St James *(opposite, above left)* stands in a quiet part of the nave surrounded by votive candles lit by pilgrims about to embark on their journey. The cloister *(opposite, above right and below)* is the cathedral's most visually arresting feature and continues the polychromatic theme of the west front. This Moorish-Spanish-influenced part of the building is reminiscent of the Great Mosque in Cordoba and a perfect example of the cross-pollination of artistic and architectural ideas that flowed between south-western France and Islamic Spain during that period. Different sculptors have patently executed the capitals as both the types of stone and subjects portrayed vary between quite stylized biblical angels to grotesque mythical creatures. Although the cloister can sometimes look rather grey, when the morning sun bounces off the surrounding cathedral walls, the coloured stones are enriched with a warm glow that instantly brings it to life.

(Overleaf) The dramatic Allier Gorges to the west of Le Puy-en-Velay.

(Below) The tiny chapel of Saint-Jacques perched high on a belvedere above the Allier Valley once served as the private chapel to the thirteenth-century castle of Rochgude, a fragment of which survives on the rocky pinnacle above. A cluster of farm buildings adjacent to the chapel are the only signs of human habitation and this isolated outpost evokes the true spirit of medieval pilgrimage. *(Right)* Saint-Privat-d'Allier is a small village set high above the dramatic Allier gorges and being just over 12 miles (20km) from Le Puy-en-Velay is used by most pilgrims on the Via Podiensis as their first overnight halt.

Conques stands on the steep side of a narrow valley above the confluence of the rivers L'Ouche and Dourdou. A narrow street lined with medieval houses climbs up to the abbey church of Sainte-Foy *(right)*, one of the most important pilgrimage churches on the Via Podiensis. The passion for relics during the Middle Ages that peaked during the twelfth century transformed this isolated place into a religious centre whose fame spread far beyond the borders of France. With perhaps the exception of Vézelay, no other place on any of the French routes has so retained the spirit of medieval pilgrimage, an atmosphere that has survived the village's escalation into a major tourist destination. Conques has not demeaned its heritage with gaudy gift shops to cater for day trippers and when the cars and coaches have departed, the village reassumes its mystical aura of centuries past. Although Conques can now be readily accessed by road, its original remoteness highlights the fact that no distance was too far, no journey too arduous if it enabled pilgrims to draw upon the perceived spiritual and healing power of a particular saint. In the case of St Foy (which translates as Faith), a young girl martyred in Agen by pre-Christian Romans in the early years of the fourth century, such belief knew no bounds and people flocked to her shrine there. St Foy's original shrine in Agen was some 125 miles (200km) further west from Conques and there are various versions of the legend regarding the translation of her relics to Conques, mostly centred around the quite common medieval practice of relic relocation, otherwise known as theft! As the fledgling ninth-century monastery at Conques was without any of the saintly connections necessary to attract pilgrims and wealthy patronage, the taking of the relics seemed justifiable and it was not long before they had the desired effect. The original church was replaced in the twelfth century by a grand Romanesque structure with an interior typical of a pilgrimage church of that period comprising wide aisles and an ambulatory to permit the free flow of worshippers around the chancel where the relics would have originally been displayed. Conque's greatest possession is the jewel-bedecked gold reliquary statue of the saint that undoubtedly ranks highly amongst the surviving treasures from the time of medieval pilgrimage and which along with many other important pieces of religious art and jewellery is now displayed in the abbey's treasury.

(Opposite, above) The church of Sainte-Radegonde in Saint-Félix near Figeac has an eleventh-century tympanum depicting Adam and Eve in the Garden of Eden and a stained-glass window of St James as a pilgrim with staff and scallop shells. *(Opposite, below left)* The wide ambulatory in the pilgrimage church of Saint-Sauveur, Figeac. *(Opposite, below right)* A recently restored statue of the apostle is the centerpiece of the altar of St James in the church of Notre-Dame, Figeac. *(Above)* A graphic portrayal of Lucifer on the tympanum of the abbey church in Conques. *(Right)* Romanesque capital in the cloister of Conques Abbey.

(Right) Rocamadour evolved into one of France's most revered sites of Marian pilgrimage and was visited by European monarchs including Eleanor of Aquitaine and Henry II, Blanche of Castille, Louis IX of France and many others. Although not on the direct route of the Via Podiensis, it was deemed so spiritually important that pilgrims bound for Santiago de Compostela would divert there after Figeac to then rejoin the main route at Cahors or further west. *(Overleaf)* The imposing fourteenth-century Pont Valentré was built over the River Lot to defend the city of Cahors. Its fortifications comprised three towers with gates and portcullises.

The abbey church of Saint-Pierre, Moissac, possesses a collection of the most beautiful and moving examples of Romanesque art, most notably the seventy-six capitals of the cloister supported on softly coloured marble pillars alternating between single and double columns that were completed around 1100. The capitals are finely sculpted with an unsurpassable array of imagery comprising numerous well-known stories from both Old and New Testaments of the Bible, scenes from the lives of the saints and representations of nature combined with other graphic motifs of pagan iconography. The single capital in the foreground of the photograph *(left)* depicts the martyrdom of St Saturnin, the first Bishop of Toulouse in southern France, who was tied to a bull and dragged around the streets of the city following his refusal to acknowledge or participate in a pagan ceremony involving the sacrifice of the animal. The Benedictine monastery was originally founded in the seventh century by Bishop Didier but the buildings associated with that era were destroyed by a succession of invaders. Moissac's later renaissance can be directly attributed to its eleventh-century affiliation with the powerful Order of Cluny and under the direction of Abbot Durand de Bredon, the new abbey church was consecrated in 1063. In addition to the cloister, the church of Saint-Pierre is also graced by a tympanum dominated by a majestic figure of Christ surrounded by the Evangelists and the Elders of the Apocalypse, all framed in a doorway comprising an array of imagery with noticeable Byzantine influences. Because neither the cloisters nor the south-facing entrance portal are particularly exposed to the elements and Moissac is removed from major industrial centres, the inevitable weathering process and airborne pollution that has affected so many other churches from the Romanesque period has been minimal. Thankfully we now live in an age where our built heritage is treasured and conserved but it does seem extraordinary that French railway route planners of the mid-nineteenth-century were on the verge of securing the demolition of the cloister to accommodate the Bordeaux to Séte line. Even though part of the large abbey complex was lost, sanity ultimately prevailed. Saint-Pierre has also had to survive a siege by the forces of Simon de Montfort during the thirteenth century Albigensian Crusade against the Cathars and massive floods that destroyed much of the city in 1930 when the River Tarn burst its banks.

(Right) The modern replica of a medieval pilgrim's gravestone marks the convergence point of three of the French routes. *(Opposite, above)* The impressive fourteenth-century collegiate church of Saint-Pierre at La Romieu. *(Below)* Auvillar is renowned for its unusual triangular village square and circular covered market, built in 1825 on the site of the thirteenth-century original. *(Opposite, below left)* The village of Ostabat-Asme was originally an important staging post for pilgrims passing through the Basque Country *en route* to the Pyrenees and Spain. *(Opposite, below right)* Saint-Jean-Pied-de-Port has long been an important resting place for pilgrims arriving from France prior to crossing the Pyrenees and as it is now served by a good rail link from Paris, the town is used by many twenty-first-century pilgrims to begin their journey on foot along the Camino Francés. Saint-Jean's name translates as 'foot of the pass' and the climbing starts very soon after leaving the town's ramparts. Saint-Jean was originally encircled by defensive walls during the early-thirteenth century by Sancho VII, the king of Navarre, but they were augmented four centuries later by the addition of a citadel and substantial ramparts.

CAMINO FRANCÉS

Saint-Jean-Pied-de-Port to Santiago de Compostela

484 MILES / 31 DAYS

The resurgence in popularity of the Camino Francés to the shrine of St James the Apostle in Santiago de Compostela has become a catalyst for the expansion and development of other pilgrim routes both in Spain and further afield. There are now links to the Camino from many corners of Europe, but regardless of their starting point, all eventually lead to the Pyrenees and the beginning of the iconic route across Spain that pilgrims have been walking for well over a thousand years. At the time of the discovery of the apostle's tomb, the Moors occupied all but a narrow strip of Christian held territory in the north. Spain at that time sorely needed a motivational driving force to launch the Reconquest and sustain its momentum during what would become a centuries-long campaign to drive the Islamic invaders back across the Mediterranean. The churches and cathedrals of the Camino Francés feature representations in glass, wood and stone of St James (Santiago in Spanish) as a humble pilgrim but more significantly as his alter ego *Santiago Matamoros* (the Moor slayer). Santiago's role as the Christian figurehead began in earnest at a battle purported to have taken place between Christian and Moorish forces at Clavijo, near Logroño in AD 844 at which he appeared on a white charger and almost singlehandedly wiped out the enemy. The numbers of international travellers making for Galicia gradually increased, not least during the time of the Crusades in the Holy Land, a period that all but halted pilgrimages to Jerusalem. Providing shelter for pilgrims still prevails as a tenet of Christian charity in many places, although there is concern that the increasing number of pilgrims on the Camino is seriously stretching the modern-day alternatives to the original hospices mostly founded by the Benedictine Order from Cluny. Some hostels are able to function on a donations-only basis but most now have to levy a charge for their beds, albeit a very modest one compared to commercial establishments. The popularity of the Camino Francés is not abating and the roads and tracks across Spain seem destined to carry tens of thousands of pilgrims each year for the foreseeable future.

(Overleaf) The hilltop village of Cirauqui cascades down on all side from the prominent outline of San Román, the Romanesque church around which the oldest part of the village was established and is still entered through a Gothic archway.

Pilgrims departing from Saint-Jean-Pied-de-Port have two route options: either the high-level Route Napoléon or the valley route *via* Val Carlos. Despite being a severe test of stamina and prone to extremes of weather, the high-level route was the one used by the French Emperor to march his troops into Spain at the start of the Peninsular War in 1808. Regardless of the physical challenge it represented, medieval pilgrims preferred being up on the bleak, treeless plateau rather than risking attacks by robbers lurking in the heavily wooded valley below. Both routes converge on the 4,265ft (1,300m) summit of the Ibañeta Pass now marked by a modern chapel and whitewashed refuge. They stand close by the site originally occupied by a monastery and pilgrim hospital before these were relocated to the more benign surroundings of Roncesvalles in 1132. The Augustinian monastery and collegiate church of Santa María *(opposite)* on the Spanish side of the pass still maintain the monastic tradition and pilgrims are now accommodated in a recently renovated three-storey hostel. The magnificent church was one of the first French-style Gothic churches in Spain and was commissioned by King Sancho VII the Strong (1154–1234). His tomb lies in the chapter house, lit by the soft hues of a massive stained-glass window depicting his great military triumph over the Moors at the battle of Las Navas de Tolosa in 1212. The Navarra ruler's own army formed part of a larger Christian coalition and the resounding defeat of the Muslim forces was an important victory within the context of the Spanish Reconquest. The original Romanesque cloister was rebuilt in the seventeenth century, having collapsed under the sheer weight of snow following a particularly severe blizzard. Two other notable buildings stand below the monastery complex, the diminutive thirteenth-century chapel of Santiago and the Romanesque chapel of Sancti Spiritus. The single bell of the former was the one originally rung from the chapel on the pass to guide pilgrims to safety through the swirling fog and clouds that linger over the summit. Sancti Spiritus was an ossuary containing the bones of the pilgrims who perished crossing the mountains. On the road leading away from Roncesvalles is a fourteenth-century wayside cross at which pilgrims made their devotions before continuing their journey.

Estella *(above)* had existed as a settlement on the banks of the River Ega long before the pilgrimage to Santiago began and even when pilgrims began flowing westwards, they avoided passing through the narrow confines of rocky valley carved out by the river for fear of being ambushed and robbed. Fortunately, the decision by Navarra ruler Sanchez Ramirez IV (r. 1076–94) to grant the town its first market charter encouraged traders to settle there and transformed Estella into a thriving commercial centre. The town consequently became an important halt on the Camino and even merited a favourable entry in the twelfth-century pilgrims guidebook, the *Codex Calixtinus*, which

said that Estella was 'fertile in good bread and excellent wine and meat and fish and full of all delights'. From the twelfth century onwards the town was adopted by the kings of Navarre as their residence and the Palacio de los Reyes de Navarra (royal palace) survives as a rare example of twelfth-century domestic architecture. The accrued wealth and status of medieval towns and cities was usually reflected in the number of churches they possessed and Estella ranks highly in that respect. The twelfth-century basilica of San Miguel *(right)* features one of the Camino's richest displays of Romanesque sculpture on its north-facing main portal.

The vineyards *(below)* originally cultivated in the twelfth century by the monks of Irache now form part of the renowned Bodegas Irache who have installed a 'wine fountain' for the benefit of passing pilgrims *(below)*. *(Opposite, above)* Los Arcos once flourished as a trading centre and important halt on the pilgrimage route, a role it still fulfils today. *(Opposite, below left)* A typical route marker on the Camino Francés. *(Opposite, below right)* The twelfth-century church of San Bartolomé is the oldest in Logroño. Its Gothic tympanum is lower than normal due to the insertion of a window above the portal.

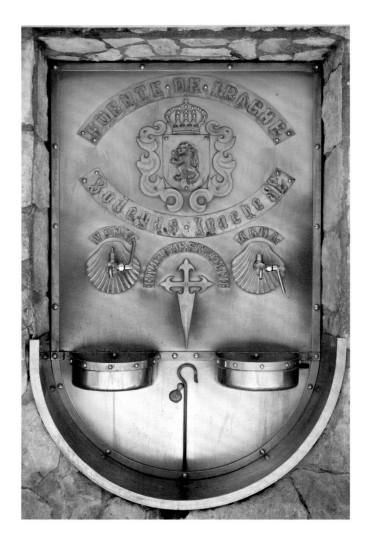

(Left) The Rioja region is renowned for its red wine but not every hectare is planted with vines and the rich soils of the plain are ideal for horticulture. This tranquil pastoral scene was the location of the alleged Battle of Clavijo in AD 844. *(Overleaf, left)* Mounted on the walls of Clavijo Castle is the distinctive cross of the Order of Santiago, founded in the twelfth century for the protection of pilgrims. *(Right)* The Church of the Assumption in Navarrete has a spectacular altarpiece thought to have been fashioned from some of the first gold arriving from the New World.

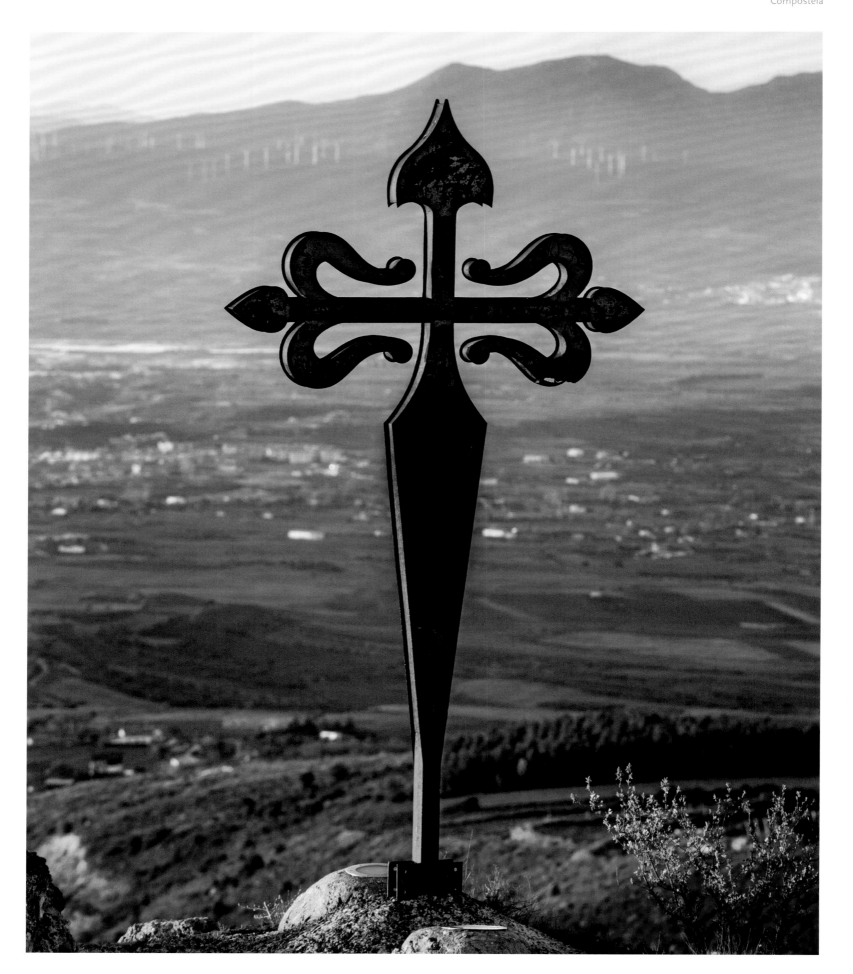

Santo Domingo de la Calzada (St Dominic of the Causeway)
is an important town on the Camino Francés and takes its
name from Domingo Garcia (1019–1109), who started his
working life as a shepherd but later undertook to devote
the remainder of his years to helping pilgrims. That vow
manifested itself in the construction of a bridge over the
River Oja and the creation of a causeway over long stretches
of boggy ground. He also fed pilgrims at a rudimentary
shelter by the river bank but as the town prospered and
grew, he was able to establish a more formal hospice next to
the cathedral and his niche statue *(left)* is set into the wall
of the Parador Hotel now occupying the site. The adjacent
church portrays a variety of architecture but is primarily
built in the Romanesque-Gothic transitional style. The
slender bell tower *(opposite)* was not added until the mid-
eighteenth century after the demise of three previous towers
built into the church. The bell tower is open to the public
and from its high vantage point *(below)* there are stunning
panoramic views across the landscapes already crossed by
the pilgrimage and those yet to follow.

Burgos was one of the most important cities of medieval Spain, founded during latter part of the ninth century by Diego Rodriguez, Count of Castille, who amalgamated several villages into one defensively secure walled town. In 1037 it was chosen as the capital of the united kingdoms of Castille and León, a title it relinquished upon the fall of Granada in 1492 when the royal court was relocated to Valladolid. Burgos thrived as a commercial centre throughout the Middle Ages during which time the city's collective wealth and the presence of so many rich patrons attracted architects, sculptors and artists from all over northern Europe. Such wide-ranging influences were ultimately manifested in the different interpretations of the Gothic style that predominates in its finest buildings, both religious and secular. The city contains more notable art and architecture than any other place along the Camino and no visitor could fail to be inspired by such surroundings. This historic city is graced by Spain's third largest cathedral after Seville and Toledo but is the only one to have received a UNESCO World Heritage designation for its architecture alone. This glorious Gothic structure was begun in 1221 on the site previously occupied by a Romanesque church. Bishop Mauricio of Burgos had lobbied vociferously for a new cathedral and in King Ferdinand III he found a deeply pious and willing ally. Both men were widely travelled and each made significant contributions towards the cathedral's composition. Mauricio had been particularly impressed by examples of the burgeoning French Gothic style he had encountered on the other side of the Pyrenees and introduced elements of that design into the cathedral. The glory of Burgos is the way that it has been designed with chapels radiating from the nave, ambulatory, choir and the two-tiered cloister. In these 'churches within a church', many of the artistic styles of several centuries are portrayed to create individual museums of Gothic and Renaissance art. One of the most stunning individual features is the open lantern vault over the transept crossing *(left)* delicately created in the Mudéjar style and towering some 177ft (54m) above the simple funerary stones of the great Spanish hero Rodrigo Díaz (El Cid) and his wife Doña Jimena. The lantern was the work of Juan de Vallejo and it is impossible to disagree with King Felipe II who opined that 'it was the work of angels, not men'.

de-Port   Logroño   León   CAMINO FRANCÉS 103

      Estella   Burgos   Santiago de
                                            Compostela

(Previous pages) The ruined medieval hilltop castle and church
of Nuestra Señora de Manzano dominate the important
pilgrimage village of Castrojeriz. *(Left)* The thirteenth-century
Gothic church of Santa María la Blanca towers above the
village of Villalcázar de Sirga but it is extraordinary to realize
that despite its current size, a lot more was lost as a result of
the Lisbon earthquake of 1755. *(Above)* The bleak but fertile
meseta to the west of Burgos is a vast upland plain given
almost entirely to cereal production but the total lack of shade
makes this a tough section of the Camino.

Sahagún became one of the wealthiest places in the region during the Middle Ages and by the twelfth century was hosting an almost unprecedented three-week-long annual market and fair. It also quickly evolved into a powerful religious centre after King Alfonso VI (r. 1065–1109) invited Benedictine monks from Cluny in France to run the monastery of San Benito (St Benedict). The far-reaching influence of the Cluniac network resulted in the abbey becoming extremely wealthy from both private donations and the income from over a hundred estates spread throughout Spain. Tangible evidence of that wealth and stature is manifested in the seventeenth-century Arch of San Benito

(below), once the south portal of the monastery church and now spanning one of Sahagún's streets. The town is unique along the Camino for its collection of Romanesque brick churches in the Mudéjar style. That Arab influenced architecture was introduced when the region became a centre of Mozarabic resettlement and so the architects, builders and craftsmen integrated their own ideas and practices into the building of new churches. The apse of the Romanesque-Mudéjar church of San Tirso *(right)* features the blind horseshoe arcading that is such a distinctive element of that building style.

León was originally a Roman garrison fortress established to house the 7th Legion. The Camino crosses the River Bernesga over a footbridge adjacent to the Puente Castro and continues directly into the heart of medieval León. There is much architecture to savour within the city's ancient centre, not least the superbly atmospheric Romanesque basilica of San Isidoro built into the original Roman ramparts. Its crowning glory is the royal pantheon containing the tombs of twenty-three kings and queens, twelve princes and other members of the nobility all laid to rest amid a portfolio of perfectly preserved twelfth-century frescoes.

However, nothing can eclipse the most elegant of all Spain's Gothic cathedrals and as one emerges from the dark streets and passageways into the Plaza Regla, the gleaming white façade presents a truly memorable sight. The cathedral is the fourth church to have been built on the site once occupied by Roman baths which themselves would have been fed by natural springs and hypocausts, a potentially less than stable foundation that probably contributed to the problem of instability experienced over the centuries. Work began on the present cathedral in 1205 and was all but completed by the beginning of the fourteenth century. The cathedral was designed in pure French Gothic style with a high nave and vast quantities of stained glass, the highest proportion of glass to stone of any cathedral in Spain. It was an equation that caused numerous structural difficulties in terms of ensuring the slender pillars had sufficient load-bearing capabilities, problems alleviated by the use of flying buttresses. The effect of having 19,375 sq ft (1,800m²) of stained glass concentrated into a comparatively small space is visually stunning, especially as the colours change constantly throughout the day with the movement of the sun. The subjects represented in some of the windows follow a logical progression in which science, nature and art occupy the lower levels, the different strata of society from peasants to nobility are portrayed in the centre with the upper levels reserved for prophets, saints and the full panoply of religion. *(Below)* The cathedral museum is housed in the cloister where some walls are adorned by frescoes painted by the artist Nicolás Francés during the 1460s. The museum collection comprises paintings, sculptures and ancient manuscripts that all contribute towards a better understanding of León's religious history and its artistic progression through the centuries.

108 PILGRIMAGE

St-Jean-Pied-
de-Port   Logroño   León
      Estella   Burgos   Santiago de
Compostela

(Above) The isolated village of El Acebo in the mountains west of León has long been a refuge for pilgrims on the Camino Francés, a tradition maintained to the present day. *(Right)* The magnificent twelfth-century castle of the Knights Templar still dominates the town of Ponferrada. The Templars were established at this strategically important site in 1178 to protect the pilgrimage route through the Bierzo region. *(Above, centre)* Monte de Gozo (Mount Joy) was the hill from which pilgrims caught their first glimpse of Santiago de Compostela and these modern bronze sculptures convey the relief and exuberance of that moment.

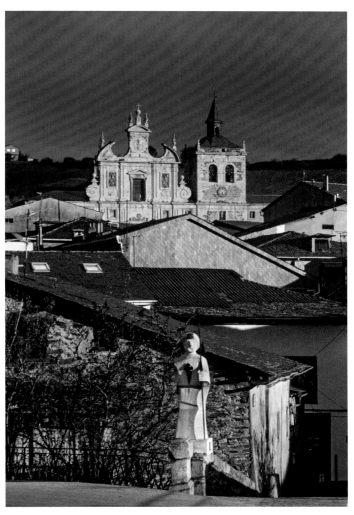

(Left) Villafranca del Bierzo stands at the foot of the Galician Mountains on the confluence of the Burbia and Valcarce rivers. One of the first buildings encountered is the twelfth-century Romanesque church of Santiago, whose northern portal was known as the Puerta del Perdón (the door of forgiveness). Pilgrims who were too sick to complete the final stage of the pilgrimage were given the same indulgences they would have received at Santiago de Compostela.

(Below) The ascent from Villafranca to the mountain top settlement of O Cebreiro is long, hard and strenuous but the views from the 4,265ft (1,300m) summit are truly magnificent.

(Overleaf) The main façade of Santiago de Compostela's cathedral is a baroque masterpiece completed in 1750 by the architect Fernando de Casas Novoa. The eighteenth-century outer stone shell encases and protects the earlier Romanesque cathedral and its main entrance through the Portico de la Gloria. The new building could so easily have been an aesthetic disaster but the combination of inspirational design, fine-grained stone and exemplary craftsmanship created a church worthy of its status as the third most important place of Christian pilgrimage after Jerusalem and Rome.

Pilgrims arriving in Santiago de Compostela will pass into the old city *via* the Puerto del Camino, just a short walk from their goal. It can be an intensely moving experience observing the emotions of pilgrims when they arrive at the Plaza del Obradoiro beneath the soaring twin spires of the cathedral. A monumental double staircase leads to the cathedral's entrance and beyond the eighteenth-century door, the cathedral's original entrance portal, the Portico de la Gloria. This apogee of Spanish Romanesque religious sculpture was primarily designed and executed by the sculptor and architect, Master Mateo. 'Obradoiro' in the Plaza del Obradoiro means 'workshops'. At the time of the cathedral's construction, the square would have been full of stonemasons, carpenters and glaziers. The sculptures surrounding the three doors of the entrance depict the Last Judgment, the saving power of Christ and of the Church and many examples of the dismal fate awaiting the damned. Leading down from the central tympanum of Christ in majesty is a column-bearing statue of the cathedral's patron, St James the Apostle. The feet of St James have become so worn away over the centuries by the fingers of reverentially kneeling pilgrims that the practice has had to be officially discouraged. Once through the Portico de la Gloria, pilgrims are drawn through the barrel vaulted nave towards the gleaming gold and silver plated altar with a centuries-older seated figure of St James as its centerpiece. Although originally reserved for feast days, the swinging of the giant censer known as the *botafumeiro* (smoke belcher) is now a more regular event. The 117lb (53kg) incense holder is hauled by eight strong men to get the censer's arc progressively higher with each swing through the transepts. The combination of a loud whooshing sound and clouds of scented smoke pouring from the vessel is an unforgettable experience. Pilgrims arriving in Santiago who are deemed to have fulfilled the necessary conditions set out for the pilgrimage are presented with the Latin inscribed scroll of the *Compostela*. Standing adjacent to the cathedral is the Hostal dos Reis Católicos, a former hospice that is now a luxury Parador. Here the spirit of pilgrim hospitality is still honoured by giving free meals to the first ten *Compostela* bearing pilgrims of each day.

VÍA DE LA PLATA

Seville to Astorga

460 MILES / 36 DAYS

The Vía de la Plata is the pilgrimage route from Andalucia to Santiago de Compostela that largely follows the original Roman road from Seville to Astorga, from where it joins the Camino Francés for the final stages. An alternative to that latter part is provided by the Camino Sanabrés, a route the branches off to the north-west after Zamora and heads diagonally *via* Ourense to Santiago. Because the Vía de la Plata is essentially all about Roman Spain, this chapter is restricted to that direct road rather than wandering off at a tangent through the green mountains of Galicia. Although one of the functions of the Roman road was to service their precious metal mining interests in the north, the romantic notion that the 'Plata' in its name refers to silver is probably not correct and more likely to have originated from either the Latin (*platea*) or Arabic (*ballatta*), words describing various types of road. The distance between Seville and Astorga is 460 miles (740km) and although it is becoming gradually more popular, the combination of extreme distance, the remoteness and sense of isolation between stages is a deterrent to many potential pilgrims. However, if one considers that a truly made pilgrimage is an opportunity for contemplation, a chance to spend extended periods away from the intrusions and distractions of modern society, then where better than on this unique road? The Camino Francés has become so overcrowded during the prime walking seasons of spring and early autumn that many pilgrims just cannot cope with the daily sprint now beginning well before dawn in order to secure a bed at the next hostel. It is certainly true that one needs at least a basic knowledge of Spanish on the Vía de la Plata but English is becoming more widely spoken in places catering specifically for pilgrims. Seville is the perfect place from which to start a journey along a route previously trodden by Roman legions, the Islamic forces of al-Andalus. Mozarabic Christians on pilgrimage to Santiago de Compostela, countless traders and the medieval artists and architects whose work contributes so much to the joy of this pilgrimage.

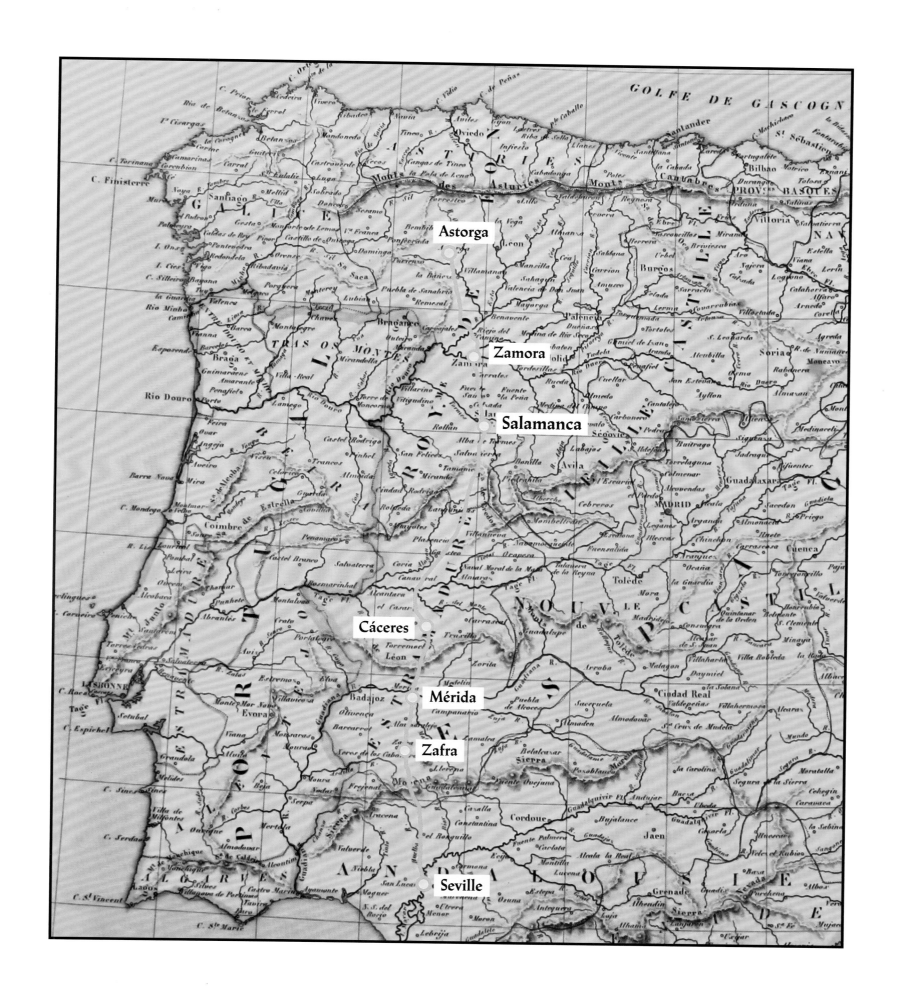

From a spiritually inspirational perspective, there could be no better time of year to begin a pilgrimage from Seville on the Vía de la Plata than Semana Santa (Holy Week). From a purely practical and fiscal angle, it is just about the worst time of year to be in the Andalucian capital, but regardless of the cost, being in Seville for Holy Week is a truly unforgettable experience. Although weather conditions can be unpredictable at that time of year, the benign temperatures of spring are ideal for walking long distances every day and Semana Santa makes a fitting prelude. Although the processions of Semana Santa are part of the Easter ritual in many Spanish cities, those of Seville are particularly colourful and intensely moving, with the many *cofradias* (brotherhoods) processing from their own parish churches through the narrow streets to the cathedral *(opposite, above)* before returning home, a slow journey that in some cases can take up to fourteen hours to complete. The larger brotherhoods may have up to 3,000 *nazarenos* (the iconic robed and hooded penitents) and it can take over an hour for them to pass by one's chosen vantage point before the first of the two *pasos* (floats) comes into view. Each parish is represented by two floats, the first featuring a statue of Christ Crucified *(opposite, below left)* or a similar Easter Passion tableau and the second a figure of the tearful Virgin Mary *(opposite, below right)*. The one part of the procession guaranteed to bring real tears to the eyes of every spectator is the moment when the float halts and the *saeta*, a heart rending lament to the Holy Mother is passionately sung in true flamenco style by a single female voice from a balcony overlooking the street. Regardless of their starting point, all the floats will arrive at the Carrera Oficial (official path), the final part of the processional route lined with banks of tiered seating. The *pasos* are carried into the cathedral though one door, where they receive a blessing from the archbishop and then exit by another door. The *pasos* are borne on the shoulders of a well-drilled team of men who have rehearsed for months. It can be heartbreaking when a procession is cancelled due to rain but as some of the statues are centuries old they cannot be exposed to water. Semana Santa demands patience and stamina from both participants and spectators alike but for all concerned it is more than worth it.

The Roman settlement of Italica was originally established during the Second Punic Wars in 206 BC and its ruins lie directly on the Via de la Plata less than 6 miles (10km) from Seville. Two of Rome's most significant Emperors, Trajan (r. 98–117) and Hadrian (r. 117–38) were born here in AD 53 and AD 76 respectively and despite having spent most of his reign in other parts of the Empire, Hadrian was a significant contributor to the development of Italica. One elite section of the town comprised several villas whose floors were decorated with complex and beautiful mosaic floors.

(Above) Zafra is frequently referred to as 'La Sevilla Chica'
(little Seville) due to its many similarities with Seville.
Moorish walls and gates surround the old town, in the
heart of which are two interconnecting squares, the plazas
Grande and Chica whose arcaded and galleried buildings
imbue the town with much of its atmosphere. The fifteenth-
century castle of the Dukes of Feria (above) has been
restored and converted into a Parador hotel. (Right) The
chapel of St James in the monastery of Tentudía contains
a magnificent early-sixteenth-century tiled altarpiece of
Santiago Matamoros by the celebrated Italian ceramist
Niculoso Pisano (1470-1529).

Mérida was established by the Romans on the banks of the River Guadiana at an important junction of the Roman roads linking Salamanca with Italica and the route between Toledo and Lisbon. The pilgrimage route of the Vía de la Plata enters the city over the first-century Puente Romana *(opposite, above right)*, the granite bridge over the River Guadiana whose sixty arches span almost half a mile (800m). At the far end of the bridge, entry to the heart of the ancient city is marked by a tall column bearing a bronze sculpture of the Capitoline She-Wolf suckling Romulus and Remus *(opposite, above left)*, the ubiquitous symbol of Ancient Rome. The name Mérida is derived from the original settlement founded as *Emerita Augusta* in 25 BC during the reign of Augustus. It thereafter quickly rose to prominence and became capital of the Roman province of Lusitania which at that time comprised large parts of Portugal and what is now Spain's western region of Extremadura. Mérida contains the most Roman monuments of any city in Spain, most of which were built by Agrippa, Emperor Augustus's son-in-law. The most imposing of those structures, today presented in an outstanding setting, is the Roman theatre *(opposite, below left)*, built in the Classical style of the great theatres in Rome. A semi-circle of stone tiers afforded seating for an audience of 6,000 with the front row being reserved exclusively for high-ranking dignitaries. Behind the stage and semi-circular orchestra is a majestic two-storey façade comprising marble columns with Corinthian capitals set on tall bases. Connected to the theatre *via* a wide passage is the Amphitheatre, a venue used to stage the more visceral events associated with Ancient Rome such as chariot races, gladiatorial combat and the inevitable fights between humans and wild animals. Although there is a reasonable representation of how it must have once looked, this arena and its vast banks of seating that accommodated over 14,000 people has not fared so well with the passage of time through both natural decay and the looting of the site for building material. Mérida is a modern city successfully living side by side with its past and because the sites of antiquity are not clustered into one Roman theme park, there are surviving fragments such as the portico adorned with the sculpted medallion of Medusa *(opposite, below right)* spread over a wide area.

An original Celtic settlement on this site was occupied by the Romans in 54 BC and initially named as *Castra Caeclii* (after Quintus Caecilius Metellus, a leading Roman Commander in Spain). Although it prospered as a Roman colony that affluence declined after the arrival of the Visigoths during their fifth-century expansion into the Iberian peninsula. The Moorish conquest of Spain that eventually delivered new rulers into the city during the ninth century resulted in one of the most significant period of the town's development. The name Cáceres is derived from its Arabic title, Al Qazris and it was the occupying Almohads who were responsible for the twelfth-century walls and some of the towers that determined the available space and scope for future development of the city. Cáceres changed hands between Muslims and Christians several times during the turbulent period of the Reconquest when the fortunes of whichever side happened to be holding the town were directly affected by both political and military events elsewhere. The first Christian repossession occurred under Alfonso VII in 1141 and the knightly Order of Santiago was first founded there in 1170 under the name of the 'Fratres de Cáceres'. The wars continued to ebb and flow until the city was finally secured by Alfonso IX in 1229 and was incorporated into the kingdom of Léon. Despite its turbulent past Cáceres thereafter began its gradual development into a centre of religious tolerance where Arab, Jewish and Christian communities all made significant contributions to the mix of architectural styles that define the city of today *(opposite)*. One such example is the Casa de las Veletas, a sixteenth-century palace, now housing the city museum. It was built on the site formerly occupied by the Alcázar of which only the atmospheric Arabic cistern remains. Although some towers still stand in the heart of the old city, many that were once attached to the mansions built by noble families during the fifteenth century as symbols of power were either demolished or truncated in 1477 on the orders of Queen Isabella I of Castille. It was a statement of intent on the part of the Catholic Monarchs to ensure that even the most powerful families could have no doubts as to where the seat of power really lay. That group of dignified but largely unadorned seigniorial mansions is just one of the elements that combine to make Cáceres such a priceless architectural treasure.

(Above) A restored section of the original Roman road climbing northwards out of the Roman town of Baños de Montemayor. The heavily sulphurated waters of the Roman baths here were renowned for their remedial benefits to sufferers of muscular and respiratory complaints and the restored site now forms the basis of a modern spa. *(Left)* The most dramatic surviving feature of the ruined Roman town of Caparra is the quadruple-arched gateway located just outside the perimeter fence of the historic site and museum. The route of the Via de la Plata passes directly through the monumental arch.

Salamanca's Puente Romano may be neither as long nor as imposing as its contemporary in Mérida but what it does possess is a skyline comprised solely of architectural treasures rather than concrete apartment blocks *(opposite)*. At first glance the cathedral towers of Salamanca appear incongruous in their differing architectural style but there is a logical explanation for that difference, namely that the architects had the foresight to eschew the accepted practice of demolishing an older building to make way for its replacement and simply retained the Romanesque original and incorporated it into the new church. The contrast in styles is remarkable and all the more informative for visitors who are able to compare and contrast the plain and solid early style with the lighter more flamboyant creation of the new cathedral that was begun in 1513 to be finally completed in 1733. Work on the predominately Romanesque cathedral was carried out through the twelfth century until its completion during the first quarter of the thirteenth century, allowing traces of early Gothic details to be incorporated into the Romanesque. The dome and its lantern are outstanding pieces of work built in three cylindrical tiers with sixteen columns allowing for thirty-two windows, all decorated with seventy-four smaller columns, in a symphony of perfect symmetrical simplicity.

Built over two centuries (from the sixteenth to the eighteenth), the architecture and decoration of the new cathedral encompasses influences from the Gothic, Renaissance and Baroque periods to create a light and spacious interior with exquisitely fine and detailed vaulting, delicate cornices and slender pillars that form part of the overall design rather than simply being a means of support. However, what does set Salamanca apart from so many other great cathedral cities are the examples of secular architecture that eclipse even the magnificence of the cathedral. Salamanca is home to one of the oldest universities in Europe, having been given a charter by Alfonso IX (King of Léon and Galicia) in 1218, a privilege confirmed by his successor, Ferdinand III twenty-five years later. The entrance to the oldest part of the university in the Patio de las Escuelas (Schools Square) features the most sublime example of Plateresque architectural design in Spain. During the early-sixteenth century, Spanish architects and sculptors perfected styles of decoration so finely and delicately crafted they were compared to the intricate metalwork produced by silversmiths, hence the term Plateresque, from *plata*, meaning silver.

The site above the River Duero (Douro) where the city of Zamora now stands has been occupied for thousands of years and developed from those early settlements as the Roman town of Ocellum Duri. Only traces remain of the walls that made Zamora the most westerly bastion of the fortified Duero line during the Reconquest, but it was a constant theatre of war between the eighth and eleventh centuries, changing hands between Moors and Christians several times. Zamora was also the focal point of internecine disputes between Sancho II, Alfonso VI and Urraca of Zamora over their respective inheritances of land and titles from their father Ferdinand I, King of Castile and Léon (r. 1037–65). It was at this time that El Cid (Rodrigo Díaz de Vivar, 1040–99) entered the panoply of Spanish history through his involvement with Sancho and Alfonso and subsequent heroic deeds in the defeat of the Moors at Valencia. Zamora is a city blessed with significant Romanesque architecture including a cathedral famous for its Byzantine and Moorish influenced dome based upon Hagia Sophia in Istanbul. It also has a collection of Romanesque churches that have managed to retain most of their original features with minimal interference from later periods.

(Above) This part of Zamora Province is called the Tierra del Pan due to the vast quantities of grain grown here. *(Opposite, above)* Alija del Infantado has long been renowned for the medicinal properties of its many mineral springs. *(Opposite, below)* The remains of Castrotarafe include a castle once associated with the Order of the Knights of Santiago. *(Overleaf, left)* Santa Maria del Azoque, Benavente, is a Romanesque church with the unusual east end layout of five apses, each with its own chapel. *(Overleaf, right)* The church of San Salvador in La Bañeza was built on the site of a very early tenth-century pilgrim's hospice.

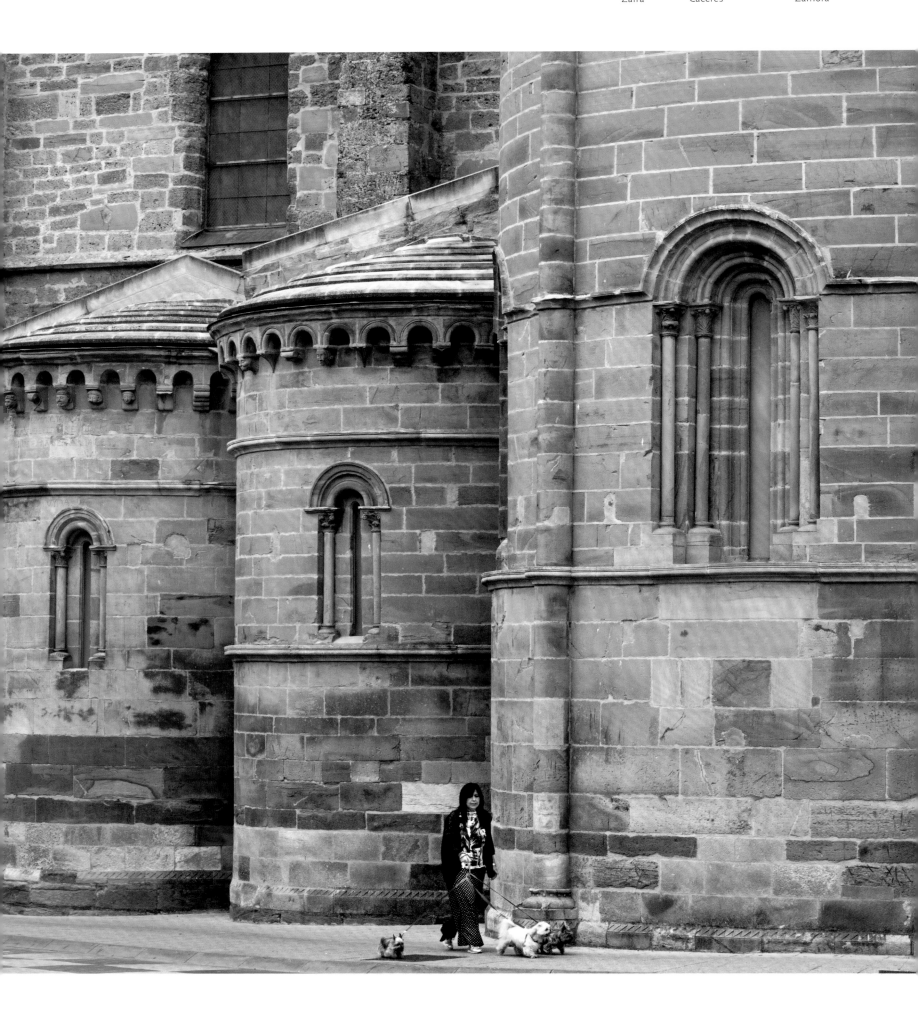

Astorga is the site of a unique architectural trio *(overleaf)* comprising solid Roman walls, a Renaissance cathedral and a late-ninteenth-century Episcopal Palace designed by Antoni Gaudí (1852–1926) The bishop's palace *(opposite)* was built from pale granite in Gaudí's inimitable style, so mesmerizingly featured in his crowning achievement, the Sagrada Família in Barcelona. Most elements of his creative genius are distilled into the neo-Gothic chapel with its intersecting rib vaults, stained glass set in pseudo-Gothic windows and a profusion of mosaics. One curious aspect is how this gleaming pastiche of a medieval palace materialized in a conservative rural corner of north-western Spain. It transpires that Gaudí was invited to take the commission by his friend, the Catalan bishop Juan Bautista Grau y Vallespinós, who was appointed Archbishop of Astorga in 1889. However, once construction got under way and the locals saw exactly what kind of building their taxes and donations to the church were funding, there was such a high degree of angst and outrage that the architect prudently maintained a low profile away from Astorga. The situation was further exacerbated by the death of the Archbishop in 1893 and so the building lay unfinished for a number of years until finally completed to the original concept by Ricardo Guerata in 1913.

The geometric lines of Gaudí's creation act as a perfect aesthetic foil for the architecturally hybrid pale red sandstone cathedral. The cathedral was begun in 1471, replacing the earlier Romanesque and Gothic buildings on the site. Although the east end and nave essentially belong to the late Gothic period and feature the customary slender columns and elegant fan vaulting, it is the later Renaissance and Baroque west façade and towers that are the cathedral's crowning glory. Astorga was established by the Romans as *Asturica Augusta* in 14 BC at the strategically important road junction of the east–west Via Traiana and the Vía de la Plata, both of which were significant trade routes long before the pilgrimage to Santiago de Compostela became a further factor in the town's economic prosperity. Astorga rapidly grew in stature as the Romans exploited the region's rich mineral wealth, especially the gold mines of Las Médulas near Ponferrada, seams that were worked to exhaustion between the first and third centuries. Once the route to Santiago became established, Astorga's geographic location at the foot of a mountain chain made it a popular staging post and at the height of this route's popularity it possessed over twenty hospices.

VIA COLONIENSIS

Cologne to Trier

149 MILES / 11 DAYS

The 149-mile (240km) Via Coloniensis runs between two of Germany's most important Roman cities, Cologne and Trier. The Latin name has been retained rather than being known by the term 'Jakobsweg' (Way of St James) given to most of the other pilgrimage routes throughout Germany. It is one of the country's vast network of thirty major routes, plus many intermediate subsidiaries, that are now fully signed with the distinctive yellow scallop shell on a vibrant blue background. They all share the purpose of navigating pilgrims bound for Santiago de Compostela across the border into France, thereafter linking up with the Via Podiensis at Le Puy-en-Velay or in the case of the Cologne route, the Via Lemovicensis at Vezelay. The more southerly tracks such as the Münchner Jakobsweg (see page 156) converge on Lake Constance and thereafter cross Switzerland on the Via Jacobi.

Having cleared the extensive outskirts of Cologne, this route charts a course over pleasantly rolling countryside before passing through the spa town of Bad Münstereifel. The landscape becomes gradually more wooded as it crosses sections of the Eifel National Park, and although the walking is not unduly taxing in terms of altitude, there are still some quite steep-sided valleys to negotiate. During its latter stages, the Via Coloniensis briefly crosses into Luxembourg to follow the south bank of the River Sauer into the historic town of Echternach before recrossing into Germany and arriving in Trier. From a purely atmospheric and architectural perspective, the mid-route highlight is the black and white, half-timbered town of Blankenheim but although all the recommended stopover locations are meritorious in their own way, the historical and religious legacies of Cologne and Trier are exceptional. First-time visitors to Trier will find a wealth of architectural treasure in Germany's oldest city, whose outstanding monuments include the huge edifice of the old city gate, the Porta Nigra. Cologne has a world-famous cathedral and enough outside bars and restaurants to tempt even the most resolute pilgrims away from the rigours of the road. Regardless of one's mode of transport, the Via Coloniensis will be a rewarding and unforgettable journey.

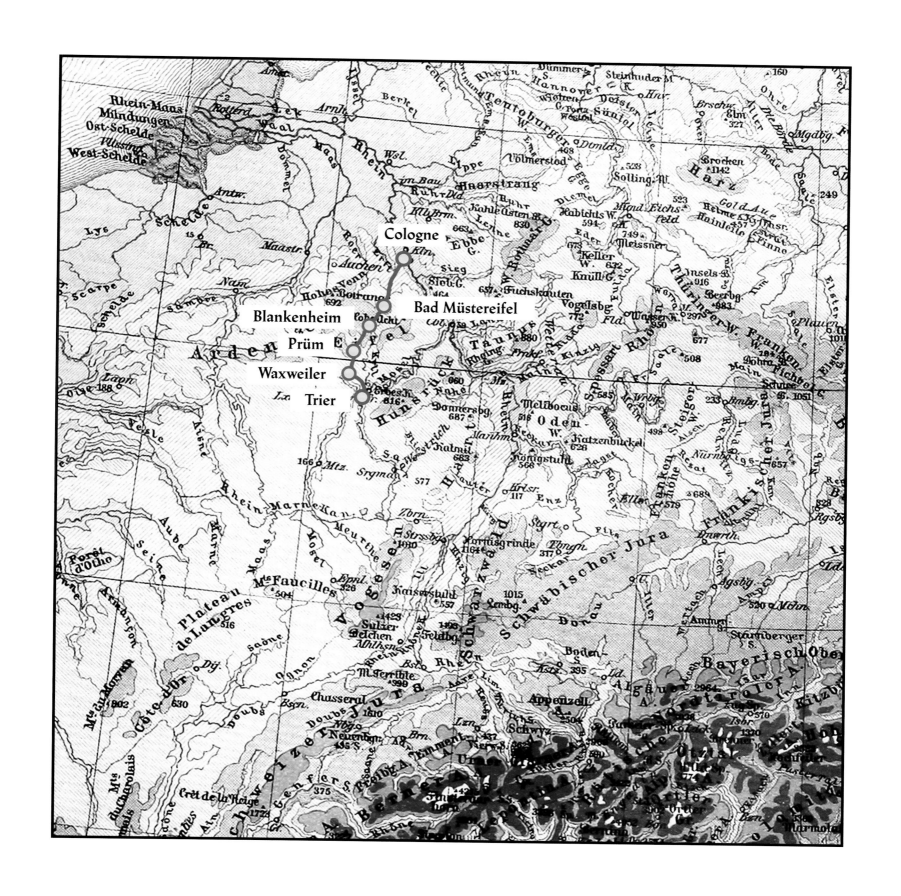

It is hard to imagine that this vast metropolis (Germany's fourth largest city) was originally a small Roman encampment founded by General Agrippa in 38 BC, subsequently evolving into a town created specifically for retired legionaries at the behest of Agrippina, wife of Emperor Claudius. It was given the rather long title of Colonia Claudia Ara Agrippinensium but was later sensibly shortened to Colonia, from which the city's current name is derived. Cologne's strategic location on the River Rhine led to a flourishing of trade and commerce during the Middle Ages when the city was a prominent member of the mercantile Hanseatic League. The semi-circular shape of the inner city at that time was enclosed within a defensive wall, with the flat side of the semicircle formed by the River Rhine. Although Cologne has now spread far beyond those original boundaries, that inner city with the majestic Gothic cathedral at its heart *(opposite, above left)* is still the focal point of Cologne. Its status was further enhanced in the twelfth century when the relics of the Three Kings (the Magi) were brought to the city from Milan in 1164 by Archbishop Rainauld Dassel. A precious reliquary shrine was commissioned from the celebrated goldsmith Nicholas of Verdun and after its completion in 1225, Cologne quickly became established as a major pilgrimage destination. The shrine *(opposite, above right)* is a masterpiece of gold and silver work encrusted with precious stones and an invaluable survivor from the pre-Reformation era that provides an insight into just how magnificent medieval shrines might have looked before they were destroyed. Although the cathedral escaped comparatively unscathed after the Allied bombing raids of the Second World War, much of Cologne's historic city centre was flattened. Most of its historic buildings and twelve Romanesque churches have been meticulously rebuilt. The largest of these is St Maria im Kapitol (St Mary's in the Capital), a Romanesque church begun in 1065 that was also endowed as a Benedictine monastery, whose cloisters were also rebuilt after war damage *(bottom, left)*. St Maria is endowed with many works of art but one of the most endearing is a fourteenth-century statue known as the Limburg Madonna *(bottom, far left)* that stands in front of the Renaissance rood screen. It was discovered near the ruins of Limburg monastery in the Palatinate region and found its way to this church during the late 1800s.

The Via Coloniensis passes directly in front of the
Augustusburg Palace in Brühl, 8 miles (13km) south of
Cologne. This lavish residence of the prince-archbishops of
Cologne was created from the ruins of an earlier fortress
by Prince Elector Clemans August (1700–61). He hired
some of Europe's finest artists and craftsmen to create an
interior of unbelievable opulence designed to impress and
the main staircase of shimmering marble and stucco work
designed by Balthasar Neumann is pure genius. Augustburg
is considered to have been the earliest and best example of
early-eighteenth-century Rococo architecture in Germany
and was awarded World Heritage Site status in 1984.

(Left) The tightly packed cluster of historic buildings and houses of Bad Münstereifel is dominated by the imposing twin-towered abbey church dedicated to saints Chrysanthus and Daria. *(Left, below)* Blankenheim is a small medieval town in the Eifel region comprised almost entirely of black and white timber-framed houses. *(Below)* A section of the Via Coloniensis near Frohngau follows a tree-lined narrow rural lane *(right)* Euskirchen was granted its town charter in 1302 but the old town hall clock tower and the few surviving medieval half-timbered buildings are sadly now becoming overwhelmed by concrete and shops.

The Via Coloniensis winds through the increasingly undulating countryside of the Eifel on the approach to Prüm, a compact town situated about two thirds of the way between Cologne and Trier. It is an important overnight halt for pilgrims and there is a detailed route map and information board in the centre of town standing alongside a metal statue of a rather jaunty-looking St James in pilgrim attire. The town's setting at the head of a steep-sided valley has restricted development and consequently its appearance has changed little in recent decades. Prüm's greatest architectural feature is the basilica of St Salvator, whose twin towers are a landmark visible from afar. This is the abbey church of what was once a powerful and wealthy Benedictine monastery. It was first founded in AD 721 by Bertrada, a Franconian noblewoman who invited monks from nearby Echternach in Luxembourg to consolidate that first religious house. It was later rebuilt and given great endowments of land and property by the first Carolingian king, Pepin III (r. 751–68). Pepin was married to Bertrada's grand-daughter (also confusingly named Bertrada) and this devout family were instrumental in spreading Christianity throughout the region. It was after the first rebuilding that it became a Benedictine monastery administered by monks from Meaux near Paris. Prüm continued to benefit from the patronage of the Carolingian dynasty, not least from Pepin's illustrious son Charlemagne who reigned as King of the Franks (768–814) and was crowned the first Holy Roman Emperor in 800. The abbey was endowed with titles and estates extending from Normandy to the Rhône and from the Low Countries to the Rhinelands. The fourteenth and fifteenth centuries were a period of decline until the abbey's fortune was revived when incorporated into the Bishopric of Trier. The original Romanesque abbey church was partially rebuilt and re-styled in 1721 with a largely Gothic interior but given a dramatic Baroque façade *(right)*. In common with most other monastic houses, Prüm Abbey was dissolved in 1803, stripped of its estates and secularized. Prüm did not fare well during the Second World War, when most of the town was destroyed or badly damaged. Upon completion of the rebuilding process, the former abbey church was elevated to the status of Basilica Minor by Pope Pious XII in 1950. It now serves as the town's parish church and the adjoining complex of monastic buildings is now a secondary school.

BASILICA PONTIFICIA

(Above) The fifteenth-century church at Neuerburg stands high above the small market town and those making the steep climb are rewarded by a vaulted interior and subtle painted decoration that imbues the church with a pastoral tranquillity. (Above, right) The village of Waxweiler nestles at the foot of a valley on the main road between Cologne and Trier and has long been an overnight halt for both pilgrims and the passengers who once used the horse drawn stagecoach services. (Right) Butzweiler's mid-eighteenth-century parish church dedicated to St Remigius is on the penultimate stage of the route.

(Left) Some of the most visually impressive parts of the Via Coloniensis pass through the Eifel National Park and throughout the route pilgrims are guided by frequent signposts bearing the distinctive yellow scallop shell symbol of the Santiago pilgrimage. The region is renowned for its pedestrian and cycle trails and this marker post above Waxweiler is a confusing collection of logos and route markers. (Below) The undulating landscape of the Eifel National Park alternates between densely wooded areas, fields of cereal crops and meadows of grazing cattle. Respite from muddy footpaths across open ground is provided by occasional farm access roads.

The heart of Trier, Germany's oldest city, lies just a short walk away from the banks of the River Moselle *(below)* as it flows past on its way to join the Rhine at Koblenz. The world-famous white wine named after the river is produced from the vineyards rising up from both banks and a journey down the Moselle on a river cruise is a much-sought-after experience. Despite its gentle pastoral setting, the ancient cranes now restored as historical monuments along the river bank bear testimony to the river's past importance as a trade route. Prior to the arrival of the Romans around 17 BC, the fordable section of the river where Trier now stands had been settled by the Treveri, a Gallo-Celtic tribe subsequently driven out by the Romans who named their new settlement *Augusta Treverorum*. Trier flourished economically and culturally to quickly become a favourite residence of Roman Emperors, most notably Constantine the Great (AD 306–37), whose contribution to Trier's architectural heritage was immense. One of the most stunning buildings from his reign is the large red brick Basilika, originally the audience hall of Constantine's palace, which now serves as the Protestant parish

church. It has been restored and rebuilt over time but only ever in the style in which it was created and so is now the largest surviving interior from classical Rome measuring 220ft (67m) long, 89ft (27m) wide and 108ft (33m) high. The other two great churches are the Romanesque Catholic cathedral and the Gothic church of Our Lady, which stand side by side on the site of Constantine's earlier great church complex. Trier's most celebrated Roman building is the Porta Nigra city gate, a vast edifice built towards the end of the second century AD, which truly conveys the power and might of the Empire. The city's three other gates were plundered for their stone but the Porta Nigra survived through its association with a Greek hermit monk named Simeon who lived there for five years and was venerated as a saint following his death in 1035. A church was subsequently created within the gate for the community of priests established in honour of St Simeon. Trier is obviously a popular tourist destination but its location off the beaten track of mass tourism ensures that both pilgrims and visitors alike will be able to appreciate this extraordinary city in comparative tranquillity.

NESCITIS·QVA·HORA·DOMINVS·VENIET.

(Opposite) A view down Sternstrasse towards Trier's Roman
Catholic cathedral from the Hauptmarkt (market square).
The enormous Romanesque cathedral was begun in 1035
and completed some 200 years later. The site was originally
occupied by the palace of Empress Helena, mother of
Constantine the Great, who subsequently built a church
there. (Left) Standing on an original Roman granite column,
Trier's market cross was originally erected by Archbishop
Henry in 958. (Overleaf) The Porta Nigra (black gate) is
the largest Roman city gate north of the Alps and the sole
survivor of the four originally set into Trier's city walls.

MÜNCHNER JAKOBSWEG

Munich to Lindau

180 MILES / 15 DAYS

The Ways of St James in Germany (die Jakobswege) are an integral part of an international network but most of them also make rewarding pilgrimages in their own right. One of the best examples is the 180-mile (290km) route from Munich to Lindau on Lake Constance, an absorbing journey providing a combination of stunning church architecture, ever-changing landscapes and access to enough Bavarian beer to quench the thirst of even the most dehydrated pilgrim! One of the more surprising features of the region is the number of abbeys and monasteries built within sight of the Bavarian Alps during the eleventh and twelfth centuries. Even though many of the monastic institutions themselves disappeared after the secularization of 1803, their legacy is manifested in the richly endowed monastic churches that were retained for parish use. Although too late for the many monasteries that were sold or destroyed during those first years of the nineteenth century, others were raised from the dead when King Ludwig I of Bavaria (r. 1825–48) sought to increase the country's spirituality by allowing the restoration of existing monasteries and in some instances, establishing and endowing new ones through royal patronage. One notable example in the context of this route is the abbey of St Boniface that was set up in the heart of Munich in 1835. As it had no means of material support (such as farmland), the King purchased Andechs (see page 160) and made it a priory of St Boniface. Most of the churches forming such an integral part of the Münchner Jakobsweg were restyled from their Romanesque and Gothic origins in the Baroque and Rococo style that took such a strong hold in this region of Bavaria. Although some of the earlier examples were executed by Italian exponents of the genre, schools of Bavarian artists soon sprang to prominence, most notably the Asam and Zimmermann brothers who were renowned for their collaborations in Munich and Wessobrunn respectively. Due to the monastic and religious heritage that survives across much of the region covered by the route, it is referred to in German as the *Pfaffenwinkel,* literally translated as 'priest's corner'.

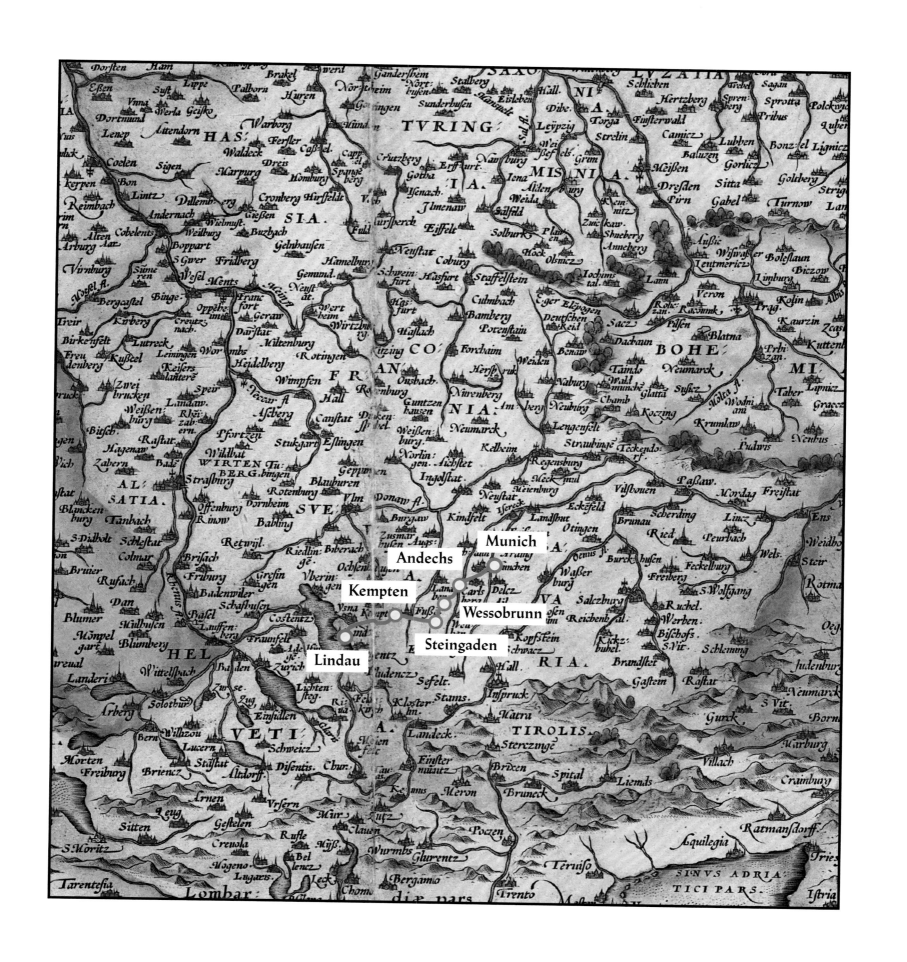

Munich is the capital of Bavaria and Germany's third largest city. One of the finest vantage points from which to fully appreciate its size and scale is the fourteenth-century bell tower of St Peter's, the oldest parish church in Munich. It can take a long time to climb the 306 steps due to congestion on the narrow staircase but its central location means that one is looking straight down into the heart of medieval Munich *(opposite, below)*. St Peter's was part of the twelfth-century monastery from which Munich evolved and the city's German name, München, is derived from the word for 'monks'. The onion domes of Munich Cathedral's twin towers *(opposite, above left)* are the city's unique visual feature that makes it instantly recognizable. However, had funding for construction of the Frauenkirche (Church of Our Lady) not completely dried up prior to its completion in 1488, the church would have been adorned by the Gothic spires originally intended. The bronze Renaissance domes, whose design pays homage to the Dome of the Rock in Jerusalem, were completed and installed by 1525. Local planning laws have sensibly restricted the height of all other buildings within a specified radius, thereby allowing untainted views of the city's magnificent skyline. During the twelfth century the important medieval salt road from mines near the Austrian border was diverted over a new toll bridge built over the River Isar. The resulting influx of trade enabled the city to thrive economically and it later became a centre of European art and culture, not least during the Baroque era of the eighteenth century when churches and palaces were transformed by the famous stucco artists and painters of the period. Two of the greatest exponents of that medium were the Asam brothers Egid Quirin (1692–1750) and Cosmas Damian (1686–1739), whose private church in Munich *(opposite, above right)* dedicated to the fourteenth-century Czech martyr St Johann Nepomuk (usually simply called the 'Asam Church') combines the very best elements of design, stuccowork and painting. The brothers wanted to follow through their own concept of a church's layout and decoration without having to comply with the wishes of a patron. Egid's dark red marble and stucco walls and the colour-coordinated ceiling frescoes painted by Cosmas combine to create an act of pure theatre, a sense of drama further exacerbated by the limited amount of natural light present. It is only when the eyes gradually become accustomed to the gloom that the true artistry of the church becomes apparent. The Asam Church may not be typical of the Baroque trail about to be followed by the Jakobsweg but it is an uplifting start to a pilgrimage through Bavaria.

The monastery and small village of Andechs are a little over 30 miles (50km) from Munich, near the south-eastern tip of Ammersee. The Baroque onion dome of the church tower rises dramatically above the hill known as the 'Holy Mountain', at a little more than 2,300ft (700m) above sea level, where the church and Benedictine monastery were built. The dedication of the church is to St Nicholas of Myra and St Elizabeth of Hungary, two saints very much associated with the ethos of charity and care that is such an integral part of the Benedictine Order. Andechs has been a place of pilgrimage since the twelfth century and although present-day pilgrims make their journey entirely voluntarily, many of their medieval predecessors had no choice. The Holy Hill was originally the site of a castle belonging to Count Berthold II of Andechs, who compelled all his subjects to make an annual pilgrimage and pay homage to the collection of relics housed in the castle's St Nicholas chapel. The relics had been brought back from a pilgrimage to the Holy Land by one of Berthold's ancestors, Count Rasso, and included a twig from the Crown of Thorns, a fragment of the Sceptre of Mockery and, almost inevitably, a piece of the True Cross. It would be easy to scorn the provenance attributed to relics brought out of the Holy Land by pilgrims and Crusaders but it must have been an overwhelming experience and easy enough to get carried away when offered a few 'priceless' treasures! Those precious relics associated with Christ (*Herrenreliquien*) were assumed to have been lost when the Counts of Andechs suffered a political downfall and their castle was destroyed in 1246. The chapel survived but of the relics there was no trace until 1388 when they were discovered buried in a chest under the altar. They became the catalyst for the building of a new church and monastery. That Gothic church was later transformed into a Rococo masterpiece with a significant contribution from the renowned stucco artist Johann Baptist Zimmermann of Wessobrunn. The lower portion of the high altar *(opposite)* prominently features the early-sixteenth-century gold and bejeweled statue of the Madonna that transformed Andechs into a significant place of Marian pilgrimage. Although the church and monastery continue to attract religious pilgrims it is currently even more popular with the secular visitors who come to sample the many famous beers brewed by the Benedictine monks.

(Above) The Maxtor is one of the fifteenth-century gates into the walled town of Schongau on the River Lech. Although slightly 'off route', it is only a short walk over the river from the Jakobsweg at Peiting. *(Right)* The ornate scrolled metalwork of the main entrance portal into the Marienmünster, Diessen, creates a fitting entrance to one of the region's most celebrated Baroque churches. *(Opposite, below)* The ferry landing stage at Herrsching is from where pilgrims leaving Andechs monastery can take a boat across Ammeree to Diessen and avoid the trek round Germany's sixth largest lake.

(*Left, centre*) Wessobrunn Abbey and the adjacent parish church of St John the Baptist are renowned for their lavish stuccowork and Rococo decoration. The present church was built during the mid-1700s on the site previously occupied by its twelfth- and sixteenth-century predecessors. Almost all the artwork, especially the ceiling paintings, give a detailed and graphic account of St John's life and murder by Salome. (*Left*) The free-standing Romanesque bell tower at Wessobrunn is the sole surviving building pertaining to the twelfth-century church. The fortified tower was accessible only *via* a ladder to a first-floor doorway.

The exterior of the former Premonstratensian monastery church of St John the Baptist, Steingaden, has remained largely unaltered since its foundation in the mid-twelfth century. Some Gothic elements were added later but following its full interior restyling during the 1770s the church essentially comprised a Romanesque shell with a richly decorated Rococo interior. A link to the church's monastic legacy is the surviving western wing of the cloister, whose Romanesque columns are supported by a Gothic vault. It is difficult to get a true perspective of the church from within Steingaden because of the tightly clustered village centre, but from the valley side one gets a true impression of the site's isolation amid the rolling foothills of the Bavarian Alps. The Premonstratensian Order was established in 1121 by St Norbert of Xanten at Prémontré near Laon in northern France. It was an even more austere offshoot of the Cistercians who had eschewed the lax manner in which the Rule of St Benedict was being interpreted by locating themselves in remote areas of countryside away from urban temptations. Most of the Premonstratensian monasteries took that ethos to an even more extreme level, as witnessed by the setting of Steingaden.

The Pilgrimage Church of the Scourged Saviour at Wies *(opposite)* is widely acknowledged as one of the finest and most complete examples of eighteenth-century Rococo religious art in Germany and richly deserving of its place on UNESCO's World Heritage Sites list. Despite being located just a few kilometers away from the important monastery and church at Steingaden, the Wieskirche stands virtually alone on an elevated site surrounded by a converging network of narrow farm roads and tracks originally used by pilgrims *(above)*. The church is directly linked to Steingaden through its founding legend. The story goes that a statue of the Scourged Christ was made for the Good Friday procession at Steingaden but the interpretation was deemed too graphic and abandoned. However, it was taken home by a local farmer and made an object of veneration for his own family. On 14 June 1738 and again the following day, drops of liquid were seen on the face of the figure and assumed to be tears. As was customary following such a miraculous event, a small chapel was built on the site of the apparition and, as word of the miracle spread, the number of pilgrims increased to such an extent that they could no longer be accommodated, and in 1746 the foundation stone for a new church was laid. If the first miracle is taken at face value then it may be suggested that two miracles should be credited to the same place because as one stands at the end of the nave looking down towards the chancel, the quality of work and the vision of design and church layout seem way beyond what even the most gifted artists might be capable of accomplishing. This masterpiece of the Rococo era was created by the brothers Dominikus and Johann Baptist Zimmermann and completed in just under a decade. Dominikus was also responsible for the outstanding abbey church at Steingaden that became his final resting place. The church itself *(overleaf)* is built around a large central space with a semicircular porch and a narrow chancel. The intention was that both shape and colour should become more intense and concentrated as the building progresses towards the high altar. From the main *trompe l'oeil* central ceiling fresco in which the closed Door of Paradise faces the empty throne of the Judge of the World down to the tiniest smiling cherub, every element combines perfectly to create a true masterpiece of design.

The capital of the Allgäu region of Bavaria, Kempten has evolved into a thriving university city but has had to endure turbulent times. It began as a Gallic settlement and subsequently a Roman one under the name of *Cambodunum*. That first town constructed of wood was destroyed by fire in AD 69, rebuilt in stone but later suffered at the hands of the Allemani tribes and relocated to a more defensive adjacent hill. When the Romans abandoned the town during the fifth century it was resettled by the Allemani but then laid to waste by the Franks. The first hint of a more stable future emerged when the monastery of Kempten Abbey was founded in AD 700 and things looked even brighter when it was richly endowed at the behest of Hildegard, second wife of Charlemagne, King of the Franks and Holy Roman Emperor. However, the Hungarians then launched a series of attacks that once again left Kempten as a pile of rubble. Rebuilding began in 941. Life in Kempten was stable for a time and in the early-thirteenth century, the Catholic Holy Roman Emperor Frederick II awarded the abbots the title and status of Dukes and granted city rights to the abbey. However, a few decades later, King Rudolf of Germany (a Protestant) elevated the non-monastic part of Kempten into an Imperial city whose inhabitants then converted to that faith. Thus there were two cities sharing the same name but existing totally apart. Ultimately, the opposing forces destroyed each other's half of Kempten during the Thirty Years War (1618–48) and so in 1652 the rebuilding began yet again! Happily, the two most significant buildings from that period have survived to the present day. These are the basilica of St Lawrence *(opposite)* and the adjoining monastery and Abbots' Residence. With its soaring twin spires and octagonal dome over the presbytery, the church may be imposing from the outside but it is the interior that deserves the superlatives. The stuccowork was carried out by Giovanni Zuccalli and the sublime frescoes by Andreas Asper. In direct contrast to the soft colours of the church, the elegant apartments and formal rooms of the Residence are the reds and oranges of opulence and excess. Although no match for the sumptuous Residenz of Munich, the building in Kempten remains one the finest examples of the Bavarian style of Rococo architecture and design.

The Münchner Jakobsweg ends its 180-mile (290km) journey at Lindau's picturesque harbour on Lake Constance (Bodensee) and pilgrims ultimately bound for Santiago de Compostela can take one of the Lake steamers across to Switzerland and thereafter continue onwards to Geneva and through France on the Via Podiensis. The old city is located on an island in the lake, connected to the mainland by a road and rail bridge and despite being a popular tourist destination, there are secluded back streets in which to escape the crowds and immerse oneself in the architectural legacy of this medieval port. The most significant landmark on the harbour front is the Mangturm *(above)*, an early-

thirteenth-century tower that served as both the original lighthouse and also formed an important part of the city's defensive fortifications. The colourful glazed tiles on the pointed steeple were a later nineteenth-century addition. Lindau's old town hall *(opposite)* was originally built between 1422–36 and was the setting for many important historic meetings. One of the earliest recorded was when Maximilian I (1459–1519) first convened the Reichstag in the large Gothic wood panelled upper chamber. The exterior was refurbished and repainted to an earlier ninteenth-century design in the 1970s.

VIA DI FRANCESCO

La Verna to Assisi

111 MILES / 9 DAYS

The Via di Francesco (Way of St Francis) is a 340-mile (550km) route extending from Florence to Rome. Unlike the Via Francigena, which traces the specific route taken by the tenth-century archbishop Sigeric, the Via di Francesco creates a pilgrimage by linking together places directly associated with the life of St Francis. This chapter does not cover the full journey but instead concentrates on the route between the two most significant Franciscan sites – the Sanctuary of La Verna and Assisi, where St Francis was born in 1182 and where he died just forty-four years later in 1226. The monastery and sanctuary of La Verna are one of the holiest places in Italy and nowhere could better encapsulate the ethos of poverty, solitude and penance espoused by St Francis. The remote mountain was donated to him in 1213 by Count Orlando of Chiusi La Verna, who had been deeply moved by the mendicant preacher's devout attitude and suggested it would be an ideal place of retreat for Francis and his followers. The original settlement probably comprised a few sparse wooden huts, and although most of the current monastic complex evolved during the following centuries, the small church of Santa Maria degli Angeli (St Mary of the Angels) was begun during the time of St Francis. La Verna lies on the fringes of the National Park of Foreste Casentinesi, Monte Falterona and Campigna and is the perfect setting from which to undertake the journey to Assisi. As it has understandingly become a popular tourist destination and can be busy at times, early mornings or evenings are the best times to appreciate fully the aura of tranquillity that pervades this remarkable place. The long descent from La Verna to Pieve Santo Stefano is the first of the nine stages to Assisi and there are some long but rewarding days ahead as the Via di Francesco passes from Tuscany into Umbria. The historic towns of San Sepolcro, Città di Castello and Gubbio are rich in architectural heritage and although Rome has to be the ultimate goal for most pilgrims in Italy, for devotees of St Francis, arrival in Assisi is reward enough.

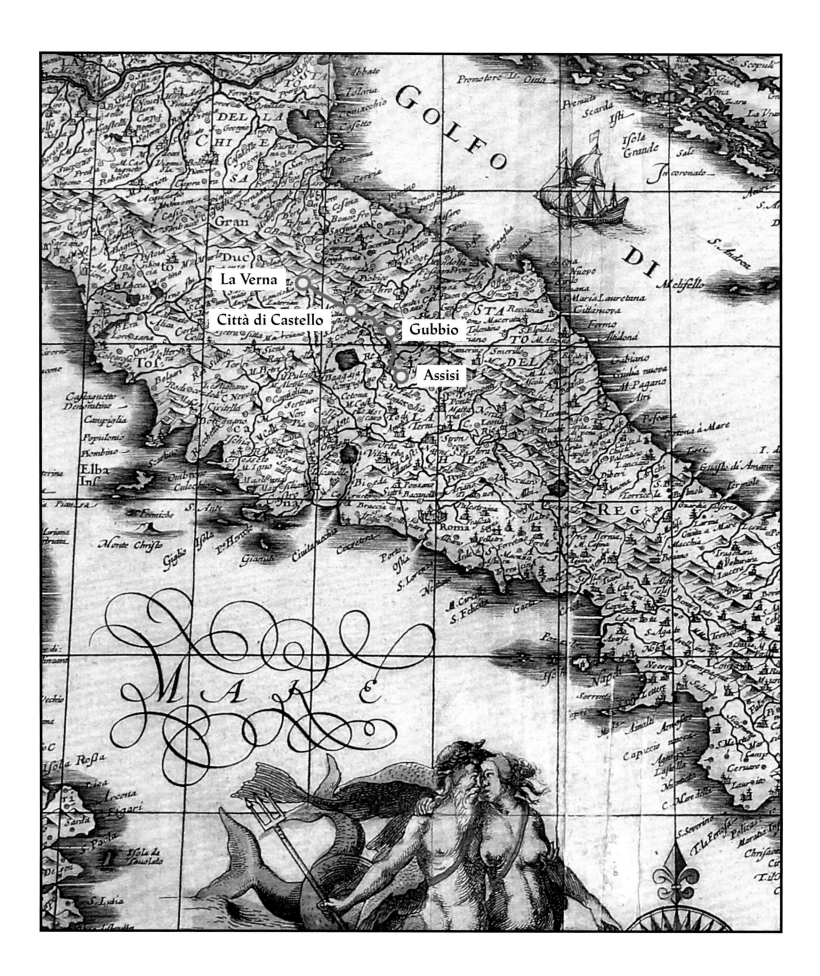

(Opposite) A simple wooden cross on the western edge of the cliffs above the sanctuary perfectly encapsulates the isolation, tranquillity and spirituality of La Verna. *(Right)* The late-fifteenth-century bell tower of the basilica and the campanile of the smaller church of Santa Maria degli Angeli dominate the compact cluster of smaller chapels and monastic building that make up the Franciscan community. *(Below)* The pilgrim route from La Verna to Assisi initially traverses the slopes of Mount Penna amid glorious beech woods where the deep silence is broken only by melodic birdsong and the occasional intrusive raucous staccato beat of a woodpecker's beak.

(*Above*) The Chapel of the Stigmata is one of the most revered places in the Sanctuary of La Verna and was the site where St Francis received the stigmata (the wounds of the crucifixion) in 1224 during an extended period of retreat, meditation and fasting. (*Above, centre*) The paintings adorning the elegant dome of Città di Castello's cathedral are by the celebrated Roman artist Tommaso Conca (1734–1822), a commission necessitated by the devastating earthquake of 1789, which destroyed its predecessor. (*Opposite, above*) The adjacent eleventh-century Romanesque circular bell tower was built when the second cathedral to occupy the site was consecrated in 1032.

(Below) Gubbio: the arches of the false basement of the Palazzo dei Consoli. Gubbio is acknowledged as one of Umbria's finest examples of a medieval town and the Consuli is its most visually striking building. Due to the town's location on the steep slope of Mount Ingino, buildings such as the Palazzo required complex support structures to compensate for the gradient. One of the most popular legends associated with St Francis is the taming of the wild wolf that had terrorized Gubbio, and this sculpted depiction of the event stands outside the Gothic church of San Francesco. (Overleaf) Assisi and the basilica of San Francesco.

All but one of the pale stone buildings and churches comprising the small medieval town of Assisi flow around the lower slopes of Mount Subasio, the exception being the mighty architectural complex supporting the double basilicas of San Francesco and adjacent friary of the Sacred Convent. The topography of the landscape necessitated the creation of an artificial 'plateau' to support the building and it is this intricate network of ever-deepening supportive arches that has made Assisi one of the most instantly recognized landmarks in Italy. The two basilicas were built on top of each other in contrasting architectural styles and completed within a surprisingly short timeframe. The lower church is almost entirely Romanesque and its massive, low interior creates an atmosphere of security and devotion. Entering the confines of the lower basilica is like walking into a subterranean kaleidoscope; the walls, ceilings and pillars of the nave and surrounding chapels are completely covered in the most sumptuous collection of frescoes. Although there are some small windows, the absence of daylight has patently helped to preserve the intensity of the colours. In complete contrast, the simple tomb of St Francis lies in the appropriately unadorned crypt of the lower basilica into which it was translated in 1230 from its original resting place in the nearby church of San Giorgio. Work on the upper basilica *(opposite, above left and right)* was begun in that same year but in a significant contrast to the lower church was built in what could be considered one of the earliest Italian interpretations of the Gothic style with an airy, bright and delicate interior *(opposite, below right)*. The upper basilica is similarly decorated with frescoes (many by the famous Florentine artist Giotto) but presented in a more cohesive and narrative style than its Romanesque partner due to the greater availability of open wall space. Both basilicas were consecrated by Pope Innocent IV in 1253. The Via San Francesco is the atmospheric medieval street leading from the basilicas towards the centre of Assisi and the Piazza del Commune. The town's Roman legacy is represented by the majestic Corinthian columns of the Temple of Minerva *(opposite, below left)*, converted into a church during the sixteenth century and now known as Santa Maria sopra Minerva. When the last tourist bus has rumbled out of the car park and dusk descends over Assisi an atmosphere of serene mysticism and deep inner peace once more prevails and regardless of one's faith, this is the perfect place to end a pilgrimage.

VIA FRANCIGENA

Calais to Pontarlier

430 MILES / 30 DAYS

The Via Francigena (The Way Through France) takes pilgrims from the English coast to the Swiss border near Pontarlier, a distance of approximately 430 miles (700km) plus the extra distance from Canterbury Cathedral to Dover, and then on through Switzerland and Italy to Rome. In these days of 'instant everything' it takes some imagination to realise that to simply receive a piece of fabric from the Pope as a badge of office, the tenth-century Archbishop of Canterbury Sigeric would have to spend almost six perilous months on the roads of Europe. It is very much to our advantage that he asked his personal clerk to make a note of all seventy-nine stages on their return journey, information which now forms the basis of Europe's most challenging pilgrimage walk.

If you stand on the cliffs of Dover above the cross-channel ferry port, the corresponding coastline of France is visible on a clear day. Travel by sea is another routine activity we take for granted but for medieval pilgrims, life afloat was not so straightforward. A basic sailing vessel was still at the mercy of the weather, especially as the winds rushing up the Channel are funnelled into greater intensity through the narrow Straits of Dover. Travellers who did make it ashore might fall foul of those who preyed upon pilgrims with heavy purses at the start of the journey. Pilgrims walking from England today will alight from the ferry in Calais, but for Sigeric the journey would have begun at Wissant a little further down the coast, because what is now a small beach resort and fishing village was once the main cross Channel port before it became untenable through sand and silt.

The Via Francigena was adopted as a European Cultural Route in 1994 and although not yet fully established as a clearly marked trail through France, the newly instigated GR145 with the red and white markers of the Grande Randonnée network is already doing its work on several sections. The countryside, villages and towns of France through which the Via Francigena passes are rich in landscape, cultural and architectural heritage and make this first of the three nationwide stages a rewarding adventure.

Arras has developed into a large modern conurbation but there is no other city in northern France where the monuments and houses of the seventeenth and eighteenth centuries form such an impressive and visually stunning array. Its architecture reflects not only the intense economic and industrial activity since the Middle Ages, when Arras thrived on the wool trade and became renowned for its woven tapestries, but also the enlightened foresight of its former magistrates who, over two centuries ago, doubled as town planners. Their influence on the style and layout of the historic city centre is reflected in the adjoining cobbled squares for which Arras is justifiably famous: the Grand Place *(opposite)* and the Place des Héros. The Flemish-style architecture of the squares is a complete surprise and the tall, narrow houses are built mostly to the same plan, with either elaborately styled or stepped gables known locally as *à pas de moineau* (sparrow steps). Given that Arras is located in the Pas de Calais region of France, it is difficult to comprehend that the region was effectively under Spanish rule from the end of the fifteenth century for almost 150 years. However, in one of the bizarre twists of European history, the Netherlands and significant portions of northern France were part of the vast Habsburg Empire, ruled over from 1555 by Philip II of Spain. It was during his reign that he issued an edict stating that all houses built within Arras had to be of stone or brick and have no overhang over the streets. He had patently been trying to negate the fire hazard associated with those towns and cities that still comprised large numbers of tightly packed wooden buildings. The market squares of Arras were gradually transformed from the Spanish Platerseque buildings into their present Flemish Baroque style. In the Grand Place, the fronts of the 155 buildings were supported by colonnaded arcades to form a continuous gallery. Following the catastrophic damage inflicted on Arras during the First World War, architects faced a monumental challenge in deciding how the city should be resurrected and the outcome was a resounding success. The squares were exactly replicated and rebuilt in the style of the originals and, in a fascinating juxtaposition, many of the streets radiating out from the central squares were reconstructed in the burgeoning Art Deco style.

The Sailly-Saillisel British Cemetery *(below)* stands on the roadside to the south of Arras and is just one of the countless similar memorials serving as poignant and moving reminders of the living nightmare that was the Battle of the Somme. This small, dignified cemetery containing over 750 graves was built by Sir Reginal Blomfield, the British architect also responsible for the immense Menin Gate memorial at Ypres in Belgium. It is almost impossible to visualize what this landscape must have looked like between 1 July and 18 November 1916 but archive photographs provide a graphic impression of the horrific conditions endured by all men in the conflict. We are now accustomed to 24-hour news coverage and live footage from the frontline of the world's current conflicts but for the civilian population back in Britain during the Great War, censored daily newspaper reports and publicly posted casualty lists were their only guide. A 77-minute silent film about the Somme was released into cinemas less than two months into the campaign and viewed by 20 million people during the first six weeks of its nationwide release. Many posters and press adverts for the film prominently featured a quote from the then Secretary of State for War and future Prime Minister, David Lloyd George, who stated that 'If the exhibition of this Picture all over the world does not end War, God help civilization!' As we stumble through the early decades of the twenty-first century, it would seem that the film did not achieve its goal because during the hundred years since its release, civilization has certainly not helped itself and, dare one say it, does not seem to have elicited much in the way of Celestial aid either. Maybe a good reason for a pilgrimage?

Laon is undoubtedly the visual highlight of the Via Francigena's journey through France. The ancient town dominates the surrounding countryside from its magnificent hilltop site set upon a narrow limestone ridge rising abruptly from the plain. The narrow plateau upon which Laon was established is 1¼ miles (2km) long and just 1,300ft (400m) wide and yet set within the confines of that small area are a majestic cathedral *(right)* and sixty-eight other buildings listed in the National Register of Historical Monuments. Although the site was probably settled in ancient times, permanent occupation began with the Romans in the first century AD. St Remigius, the influential Bishop of Reims, brought Christianity to the city of his birth and elevated it to the rank of bishopric early in the sixth century. Laon's natural defensive potential and geographical setting within France attracted the attention of the ninth- and tenth-century Carolingian kings who made it their capital for over 150 years until the death of the last monarch, Louis V in 987. The seat of power was thereafter removed to the Île de France with the accession in that same year of Hugh Capet, the first of the Capetian dynasty, whose kings ruled until 1328. The cathedral of Notre-Dame *(right)* was begun in 1150 and is an outstanding example of the earliest Gothic-style churches built during the transitional period away from Romanesque architecture. The west front is adorned by three deep set portals each with its own sculpted narrative with the central one being dedicated to the Virgin. One feature unique to Laon are the giant carved oxen adorning the towers of the west façade in representation of the twelfth-century legend about a yoke of oxen struggling to haul a load of stone up the steep hill who were suddenly aided by a mysterious third beast that disappeared as soon as the cart reached the summit. Standing next to the cathedral and now housing the tourist office is the Hôtel Dieu, the oldest extant example in France of a hospital for pilgrims and paupers. It was built in 1170 and still possesses its glorious vaulted undercroft. Substantial portions of the thirteenth-century ramparts are still intact and also worthy of exploration are the underground passages created from the old limestone quarries that have served as a medieval prison and an integral part of the city's defence system.

Reims was an important city of the Roman Empire whose population in the third century AD numbered around 80,000. The cloth trade brought increased prosperity in the Middle Ages and the city's name is now synonymous with one of France's greatest exports – champagne. Reims has a significant place in the nation's religious and political history dating back to the late-fifth century, when St Remigius converted and baptised Clovis, King of the Franks and 3,000 of his warriors. The city took its name from that influential early Christian church leader although when Archbishop Sigeric passed through on Stage LXX (70) of his epic journey, it was noted as 'Rems'. The bishop's tomb was initially housed in a small chapel within a Benedictine monastery built on the site in 800 but was soon incompatible with the increasing numbers of pilgrims. The current basilica of Saint-Remi was begun in 1079 to house the bishop's tomb and the Romanesque style from that first period was augmented by later Gothic elements. The twelfth- and thirteenth-century stained-glass windows of the choir (below) create a crown of light over the saint's tomb that now sits behind the high altar.

The 'Smiling Angel of Reims' is probably the most photographed feature of Notre-Dame cathedral but its location on one of the entrance portals not only causes congestion but also creates a very real risk of injury from 'selfie-sticks'! However, the angel is just one element in the sumptuous array of sculptures adorning the exterior that create a fitting prelude to one of the most perfect examples of a thirteenth-century Gothic cathedral. The interior is marked by an elegant lightness of construction and one of the most beautiful rose windows of any church. The builders of Notre-Dame modelled it on the cathedrals of Laon and Chartres and although the latter is justifiably famous for its glass, Reims has an equally magnificent portfolio of the glazier's art. Notre-Dame has witnessed the coronation of twenty-five French kings beginning with Louis VIII the Lion in 1223. One of the most notable was the crowning of Charles VII in July 1429 in the presence of Joan of Arc, following the French victory over English forces at the siege of Orléans.

(Above) Châlons-en-Champagne lies on the ancient Via Agrippa leading from Milan up to the English Channel. The former collegiate church of Notre-Dame-en-Vaux was a popular site of Marian pilgrimage and constructed mainly in the Romanesque style towards the end of the twelfth century. (Above right) The heart of Châlons-en-Champagne comprises many ancient half-timbered buildings.
(Right) Recycled tombstones have been used to create the steps leading down into the nave of the church of Saint-Pierre in Bar-sur-Aube.

(*Left*) The Military Academy in Brienne-le-Château was attended by a ten-year-old Napoleon Bonaparte between 1779–84. It was a strict school administered by Benedictine monks where traditional lessons were combined with basic military topics. Upon successful graduation, Napoleon went to the more advanced Military Academy in Paris. The bronze statue of a youthful Bonaparte was erected as a reminder of his past links with the town. (*Below*) One of the arrow-straight tarmac sections of the *Chemin des Romains* which in places continues as a more authentic gravel track *en route* to Brienne-le-Château.

(*Previous pages*) Langres was originally a Gallo-Roman fortified settlement named *Andematunnum* established on a limestone outcrop. Its strategically important location at the intersection of several ancient roads resulted in a centuries-long state of self-preservation, the evidence of which is clearly visible in the varied styles of architecture employed in the towers and gates that are still part of the 2¼-mile (3.5km) ramparts encircling the city. The height of the ramparts above the dramatic countryside of the Franche-Comté makes them a good vantage point but they must have seemed an extremely daunting prospect to anyone below with hostile intent.

(*Left and below*) Langres Cathedral is dedicated to St Mammes, a comparatively obscure third-century martyr from Caesarea. The cathedral was begun in about 1141 and the width of the ambulatory (*below*) signifies a church needing to accommodate many pilgrims, and once the relics of the saint were transferred from the Holy Land during the early-thirteenth century, Langres did indeed become an important place of pilgrimage. The classically inspired towers (*opposite*) were part of a mid-eighteenth-century restoration and the adjacent roof provides an excellent example of the glazed polychromatic tiling that are such a distinctive feature of this region.

Besançon is the capital of Franche-Comté and the oldest part of the city occupies a naturally defended site in a tight oxbow loop of the River Doubs that resembles an inverted carafe when viewed on a map. The 'neck' of the vessel is protected by one of the most impressive citadels designed and built by the prolific military engineer Sébastien Vauban (1633–1707) during the reign of Louis XIV. Some of the rocky outcrops above the steep-sided valley carved out by the Doubs are also fortified, confirming Besançon's importance as strategic location on the important trans-Alpine trade route linking Italy with France and the Rhine. The city's history extends back to the Gallo-Roman period when it was known as *Vesontio*. One important legacy of the Roman era is the Pont Battant, a bridge that for centuries was the sole crossing point over the river and led directly into the heart of the city along a dead straight road now called the Grand Rue. To say that Besançon is just one big museum may sound derogatory but rather points out that much of the old city is a pedestrian zone and the elegant pale stone buildings simply exude an aura of history, irrespective of

whether or not they house one of Besançon's many actual museums. Regardless of whether one is a military strategist or a photographer, height is always an advantage and the views down into the city from the early-ninteenth-century fort of Bregille were reward enough for the stiff climb. The cathedral of Saint-Jean is the last building on Grand Rue before it snakes its way up through trees to the citadel. Because it does not occupy a central location, the strength and colour of the cathedral's tower are seen to better advantage from above. The cathedral houses several impressive artworks by Florentine painters but its greatest treasure is an astronomical clock. It was made between 1857 and 1860 by Auguste-Lucien Vérité and contains 30,000 parts. It performs the normal clock functions on the church tower but also has sixty-two other dials conveying an extraordinary amount of information regarding astronomical movements, tide tables and the time in sixteen other worldwide locations. Besançon has one of the best 'browsing' cultures on the Via Francigena and from the old riverside warehouses to the dour ramparts of the citadel it is a city to savour, especially as the food is outstanding too.

(Opposite) The cathedral of Saint-Jean and the Porte Noire Roman triumphal arch create an interesting architectural juxtaposition spanning over a thousand years. The second-century arch was built during the time of Emperor Marcus Aurelius to celebrate victories over the Parthians but sadly many of the detailed relief sculptures have badly weathered over time. *(Left and above)* The Granvelle Palace was originally built for Nicolas Perrenot de Granvelle (1486–1550), chancellor to Emperor Charles V. The arcaded mansion now houses the outstanding Musée de Temps (Museum of Time).

Pontarlier's most notable structure is the eighteenth-century arch of Porte Saint-Pierre *(above)*, rebuilt after the disastrous fire of 1736 that destroyed a large part of the town. The campanile and clock were later additions at the behest of the locals but whether it was an issue of available space or a simple oversight, only the first two words of the French motto *liberté et égalité* have been engraved on its façade: *fraternité* did not make it. *(Opposite, above left)* A niche statue of St John in the portal of Pontarlier's Saint-Bénigne church with the famous *Vox Clamantis in Deserto* (a voice crying out in the wilderness) inscribed below. *(Opposite, above right)* Saint-Bénigne is a composite of many periods initially constructed on the site of an earlier eleventh-century

church but has had to endure numerous restorations as a result of conflict and fire. The tower is surmounted by a distinctively shaped glazed tile dome typical of the Franche-Comté region. *(Opposite, below)* Until the infamous alcoholic drink was banned in 1915, Pontarlier had been the home of absinthe production. The distilleries first opened by Henry Pernod in 1805 now produce more benign versions without the original's infamous wormwood.

VIA FRANCIGENA
Pontarlier to the Great St Bernard Pass

114 MILES / 10 DAYS

The Via Francigena's route through Switzerland may be shorter than the French and Italian stages but the Swiss can nevertheless boast ownership of the most iconic landscape feature on the pilgrimage – the Great St Bernard Pass. This leg of the route also encompasses one of the most beautiful stretches of scenery as it winds alongside Lake Geneva through the vineyards of the Lavaux. The route through Switzerland is signposted as Route 70, and as both the name and pilgrim logo are absent it can be confusing at a busy intersection. Switzerland's predominant natural features of lakes and mountains proved a daunting challenge for medieval travellers, traders and pilgrims bound for Rome or the Holy Land but despite the perils of traversing mountains, chinks in the seemingly impregnable wall of the Alps have been exploited since prehistory. The French-speaking canton of Vaud, which carries the Via Francigena from the French border to Lausanne, is one of the twenty-six cantons (counties) of Switzerland that are essentially small, self-governing republics with their own coats of arms. They all eventually combined to form the Swiss Federation, represented on Swiss coins by the Latin *Confoederatio Helvetica*, the initials of which (CH) are used as the country's international identification on car number plates. *Helvetica* is derived from the Helvetii, one of the earliest tribes to settle in Switzerland and whose defeat by Roman armies under Julius Caesar in 58 BC led to the region becoming the Roman Province of Helvetia around five decades later. Helvetia's geographical location compelled the Romans to undertake a large-scale construction programme of fortifications and roads: the pass over the Alps that was to become the Great St Bernard was initially named *Mons Jovis*, or in French *Mont Joux*, after the temple to Jupiter erected on the summit. Switzerland's medieval history is a complex and turbulent period of both inter-state and international conflict, the latter finally ended by the signing of the Peace of Westphalia in 1648, a treaty that not only signified the end of Europe's long running Wars of Religion but also officially acknowledged Swiss independence and neutrality.

(Above) The Via Francigena's passage from France is an
unheralded affair through a deserted border and customs
post. However, as the path winds its way through alternating
meadows and pine forests *en route* to Sainte-Croix, the
landscape and architecture gradually begin to feel more
like Switzerland. *(Opposite)* Orbe originated as a Roman
settlement named Urba which, during the Middle Ages,
developed as two separate settlements on either side of
the river from which the town derives its name. They
were united in the fifteenth century by the building of the
humpback bridge, the oldest of its type extant in Switzerland
today.

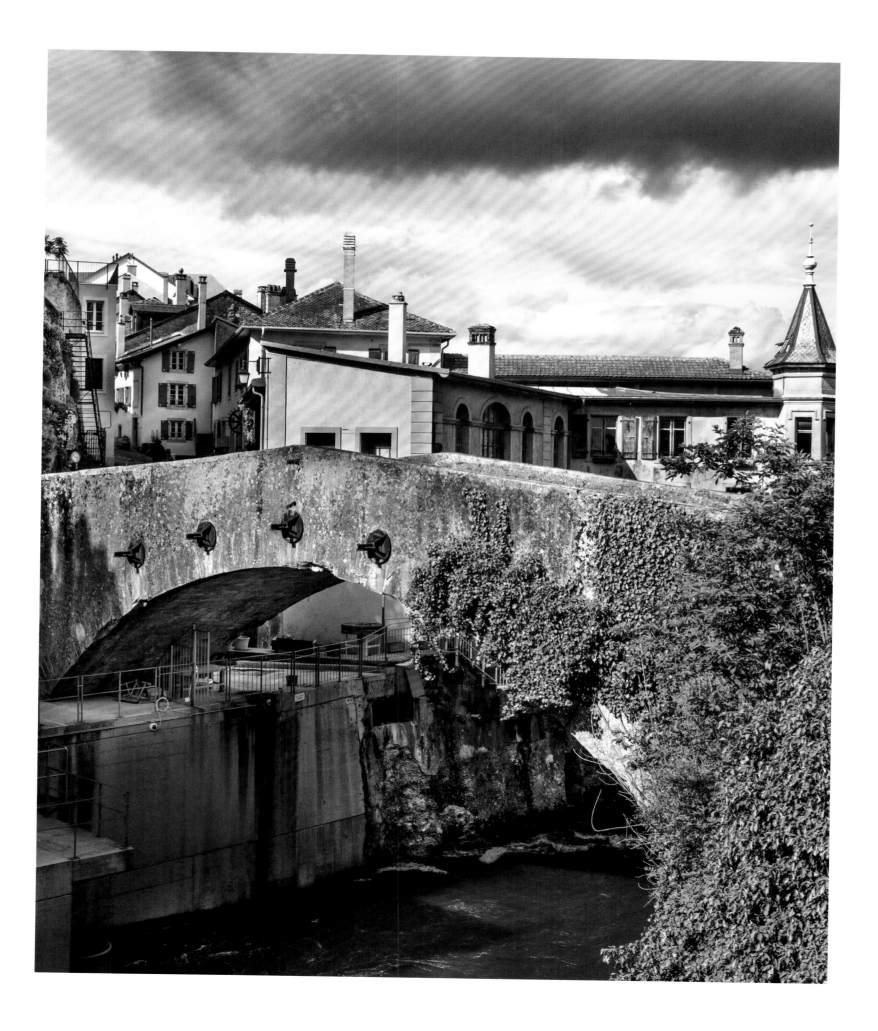

The narrow streets of Lausanne's oldest quarter *(opposite)* slope steeply down towards the city's newer areas and the shores of Lac Leman (Lake Geneva). Lausanne originated from the Roman settlement named *Lousanna* founded in 15 BC. During the Middle Ages, the city was relocated to a higher, more defensible position and it was from there that the metropolis spread over three hills and evolved into the city of today. Notwithstanding the fact that the Alps formed a natural barrier rendering communication and trade more difficult, the gradual opening up of the Great St Bernard Pass ensured that the city thrived on its position on the north–south route between hubs such as Italy's Mediterranean port city of Genoa and Northern Europe. Lausanne is Switzerland's fourth largest city, capital of the canton of Vaud and the headquarters of the International Olympic Committee. Regardless of whether one arrives in Lausanne on foot as a pilgrim or as a tourist by other means of transport it can be a daunting prospect for the first-time visitor. There is a lot to see and admire but in essence Lausanne can be distilled into two contrasting highlights: the old city and the lakeshore. The oldest part of Lausanne is also one of its highest points and the cathedral's distinctive bell tower serves as not only a prominent landmark but also the vantage point from where the centuries-old tradition of the 'night-watch' is still enacted every night when the hours are called out between 10 p.m. and 2 a.m. Every corner of the city is visible from the 245ft (75m) tower and the job of the night watchman was to raise the alarm if and when any fires broke out amid the tightly packed streets of medieval wooden houses. Lausanne's lakeshore is based around what was once the fishing port of Ouchy but is now transformed into a pedestrianized area of shaded quays and immaculate gardens offering spectacular views towards Vevey and Montreux at the eastern end of Lake Geneva from where the Via Francigena makes its way up and over the Alps. Pilgrims could save two days by taking one of the traditional paddle steam boats over to Montreux but in so doing would deprive themselves of a walk through one of the region's greatest landscape features: the vertiginous vineyards of the Lavaux (see page 214).

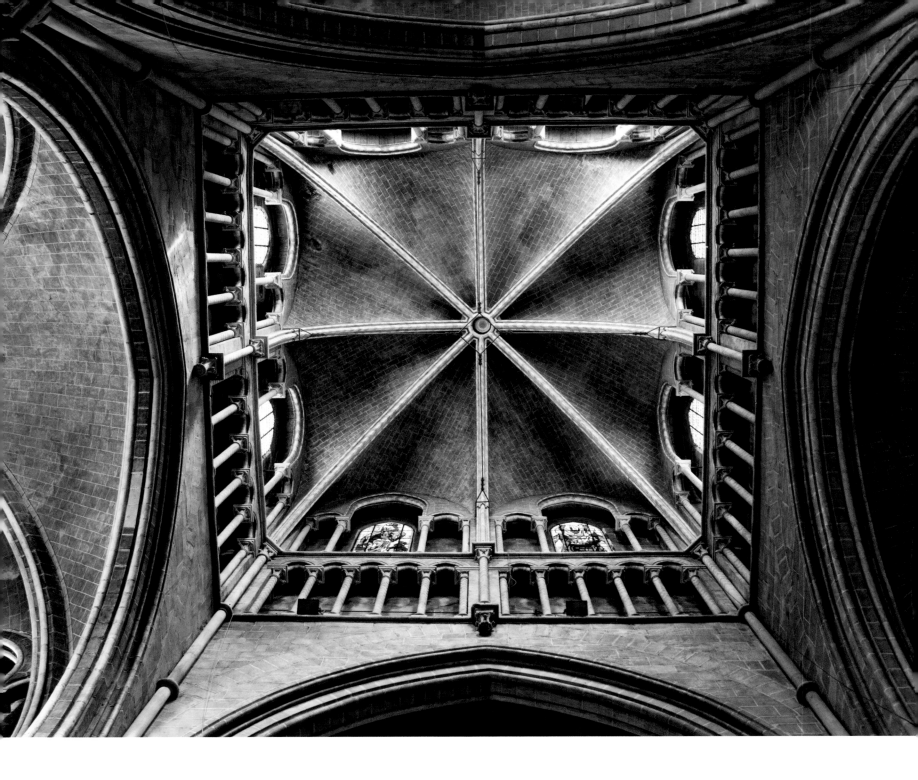

(Above) The crossing tower of Lausanne Cathedral perfectly
encapsulates the elegant style of Switzerland's finest Gothic
building. Work on the new church began in 1170, replacing
an earlier Romanesque building which itself had been
erected on the site of a ninteenth-century Carolingian
basilica. The new cathedral church was consecrated by
Pope Gregory X in 1275. (Opposite) This depiction of the
Assumption of the Virgin Mary forms part of Lausanne
Cathedral's lavishly sculpted and painted south portal
created between 1215–30. Although not desecrated during
the Reformation, the portal was whitewashed. It has since
been painstakingly restored to reveal its original colouring.

(Left) The vineyards of the Lavaux between Lausanne and Montreux have been cultivated on Lake Geneva's precipitous northern shore since the eleventh century and were designated a World Heritage Site in 2007. *(Right)* The abbey church of Saint-Maurice stands huddled against an almost sheer rock face. The first church was built to honour Maurice, a Roman commander who was martyred around AD 300 for refusing to kill opposing Christian soldiers. *(Below)* Bourg-Saint-Pierre is the final Swiss village *en route* to the summit of the Great St Bernard Pass. It originally had a fourteenth-century castle and a hospice to care for pilgrims.

The Great St Bernard (8,114ft/2,473m) is the third highest Alpine pass in Switzerland and runs between Martigny on the Swiss side and Aosta in Italy. Although the Romans were the original road builders, they were certainly not the first to exploit that natural breach in the ridge linking the highest Alpine peaks and it was used by Celtic tribes and traders long before the expansion of the Roman Empire into northern Europe. This is a bleak place that only briefly loses its snow cover during the height of midsummer and the road pass is generally closed from October to June. However, even though there is no access for vehicles, the doors of the hospice are never locked and anyone making the ascent on skis or with snowshoes will find refuge for the night. Both the pass and hospice derive their name from St Bernard of Menthon, a priest from Aosta who devoted his life to bringing Christianity to the pagan Alpine tribes and caring for the welfare of travellers and pilgrims. The bronze statue of St Bernard *(opposite)* overlooks the hospice he founded midway through the eleventh century, which has remained in continuous use up to the present day, now run by non-monastic Canons Regular who follow the Rule of St Augustine. Ever-increasing demand for accommodation resulted in the adjoining *auberge* being added in the twentieth century but only the hospice remains open throughout the year. The name of St Bernard is now shared by the huge dogs bred by the monks from the seventeenth century although it was not until 1888 that the breed then known as Alpine Mastiffs were renamed. Postcards of the dogs will invariably show a small brandy barrel slung around their necks, an image that can be attributed to the imagination of English Victorian artist, Sir Edwin Landseer. Pilgrims on verge of dying from hypothermia might need more than brandy to revive them and the ancient Mortuary Chapel standing a discreet distance from the hospice is a reminder that there were many who did not make it over the pass and whose bodies were placed there to mummify in the cold. *(Overleaf)* Walking the final kilometre of the Via Francigena below the Great St Bernard summit is a humbling experience, probably treading on the very stones that had carried Sigeric and his entourage to and from Rome.

VIA FRANCIGENA
Great St Bernard Pass to Rome

674 MILES / 50 DAYS

Pilgrims heading towards Rome who have walked up from the Swiss side of the Great St Bernard Pass and spent the night at the hospice will be within touching distance of Italy when they set out the next morning and the first Italian espresso of the day will be just a short stroll away in the bar of the Hotel Italia. The route heads past the small summit tarn and a short detour up past the statue of St Bernard leads to a vantage point from which the view is truly awesome. The vast steep-sided green bowl falling away from the summit plateau is framed on the right by the jagged 13,000ft (4,000m) peaks of the Mont Blanc massif and, far down in the distance to the left, the thickly forested valley taking the Via Francigena to Aosta. It was the return leg of Sigeric's epic journey that was documented by his clerk and even though the archbishop's crossing of the Alps was over a thousand years ago, he was able to follow the tracks forged by the ancient Celtic tribes and the more substantial road subsequently laid by the Romans to ease the passage of military traffic heading to and from their province of Gaul. Napoleon and his army made one of the most famous crossings of the Great St Bernard *en route* to defeating the Austrians at the Battle of Marengo in 1800. It inspired some graphic paintings from contemporary artists including Jacques-Louis David, whose flamboyant equestrian portrait of Napoleon with swirling crimson cloak on a rearing horse could not have been much further from reality. The French general would been led over the pass on a sure-footed mule by a local guide rather than a prancing thoroughbred horse. The distance from the Col du St Bernard to Aosta is approximately 19 miles (30km) and if pilgrims opt to complete that stage of their journey without an overnight halt, they will have made a descent of almost 6,550ft (2,000m) from snow-capped Alpine peaks to sun-drenched vines and shed many layers of clothing in the process.

Even though the walker's route on the Italian side of the Great St Bernard takes a more direct line than the long sinuous hairpin bends of the tarmac road, the gradient is never severe and the steeper sections are eased by the gentle serpentine loops previously trodden by the pack animals of merchants and tradesmen prior to the road's completion in 1905. Transhumance is still part of the annual farming cycle in the Alps and even though the summer grazing season is shorter than ideal, every day that the livestock are fed by nature is one less for the farmer to provide fodder.

Aosta was established in 25 BC by the Romans, after they wrested it from the Alpine Gallic Salassi tribe, many of whom were either slain or put into slavery. The city's current name has evolved from its original title of Augusta Praetoria in honour of Emperor Augustus (27 BC–AD 14), and although modern development sprawling outwards into the valley is unsightly, Aosta has retained its Roman heart and is a joy to explore on foot. The Roman settlement with its geometrical grid layout of streets is still encompassed within significant surviving segments of the original walls. Although Italian is almost universally spoken it was not so long ago that Aosta was bilingual and a French *patois* was commonly used by the locals, a reflection of the city's fluctuating medieval history when it was once part of the Duchy of Burgundy. Even when back under the rule of the Italian Savoy kings, the tradition of bilingualism was not only accepted but actively encouraged.

The main street leads towards one of Aosta's impressive Roman architectural treasures, the Porta Praetoria. This was the original triple-arched, double gateway into the city comprising two smaller outer arches for pedestrian use and a higher central one to accommodate wheeled traffic. Standing further east beyond the gate and now somewhat marooned on an island at a busy traffic intersection is the Arch of Augustus *(opposite)*, a triumphal arch decorated with ten Corinthian columns built to celebrate victory over the Salassi. The roof was a later addition in the early part of the eighteenth century.

The name of the street linking the Porta Praetoria and the Arch of Augustus is the Via Sant'Anselmo and in the context of the Via Francigena it is an extraordinary coincidence that St Anselm (1033–1109), one the most important and influential early medieval Archbishops of Canterbury, should have been born here. The ensemble of the collegiate church of Sant'Orso, its Romanesque campanile and cloister are undoubtedly the most moving religious buildings in Aosta and worthy of an extended visit. The church was reconstructed towards the end of the fifteenth century in late Gothic style but retains its eleventh-century crypt with Roman columns. There are also substantial traces of very rare eleventh-century Ottonian frescoes still visible high up in the church. The cloisters date from 1133 and have some of the finest carved Romanesque capitals in Italy.

Fenis Castle *(above)* dates back to the thirteenth century
and was built by the Challant family, Dukes of Aosta. The
famous façade of today's castle is an early-twentieth-century
restoration of the original and is now a museum. *(Above,
right)* The region around Vercelli is renowned as one of
Europe's largest rice producers and in late summer the rice
paddies turn golden as the grains ripen. *(Right)* Pont-Saint-
Martin. This single-arch Roman bridge dates back to the first
century BC. Its 115ft (35m) span crosses the River Lys and for
centuries remained the sole means of crossing the torrent.

(Left) A restored section of the Gaul Consular Roman road at Donnas, 2¼ miles (3.5km) west of Pont-Saint-Martin. Despite being only a short length, this example was cut from the solid rock face and perfectly exemplifies the skill and prowess of those charged with Rome's civil and military engineering projects. *(Below)* Vercelli's old market place, the Piazza Cavour is dominated by the red brick Torre dell'Angelo and the white marble statue honouring the Italian statesman Camillo Benso di Cavour (1810–61), the Kingdom of Italy's first prime minister under Victor Emmanuel II. *(Overleaf)* Pavia, the Ponte Coperto at sunset.

Pavia was established as a Roman military camp around 220 BC and the grid formation of the streets in the oldest part of the city is a legacy of the traditional garrison layout. Pavia was originally named *Ticinum* after the River Ticino (a tributary of the Po) on whose banks the city is located. In the sixth century, the city became the capital of the Lombards and hosted the coronations of such key historical figures as Charlemagne (774) and Frederick Barbarossa (1155). The Via Francigena's route into Pavia affords the best possible approach to the city, crossing the river *via* the iconic covered and arcaded Ponte Coperto with its small central chapel. The Roman bridge over the Ticino was eventually replaced during the mid-fourteenth century and it was that medieval structure which suffered damage during the Second World War and was replaced in 1951. Pavia rises up from the far bank, its skyline dominated by the duomo's imposing 318ft (97m) high cupola. The duomo may be the largest church in Pavia but there are many other wonderful churches to explore. The late-fourteenth-century Carmelite church of Santa Maria del Carmine has an interior exuding an atmosphere of elegance and calm, its wall adorned with impressive fifteenth-century frescoes *(opposite, above left)* and one must also mention the gloriously named San Pietro in Ciel d'Oro, a twelfth-century church significantly restored at the end of the ninteenth century, which is the burial place of St Augustine.

However, for sheer architectural beauty and a sense of history, San Michele Maggiore has to take pride of place. Contemporary writers in the seventh century cite the existence of a church dedicated to Michael the Archangel on this site and although that church was destroyed in the early eleventh century it was rebuilt as an outstanding example of the Lombard-Romanesque style and re-consecrated in 1155 *(opposite, above right and below)*. Pilgrims on the long road to Rome will no doubt find many towns worthy of more than a cursory glance but Pavia should be a compulsory two days rest. The city is obviously an important stage on the Via Francigena but is also yet another Italian city with direct links to Canterbury because St Augustine (buried here) was the first Christian Archbishop of Canterbury in AD 597 and Lanfranc (born here) was appointed to that same post by William the Conqueror in 1070.

The summit of the Cisa Pass may be only a modest 3,410ft
(1,040m) but on both the way up and the 12½ mile (20km)
descent to Pontremoli, the terrain over which pilgrims
on the high-level route must walk is tough going, but
fortunately there is a less strenuous option available by
following rural roads. Nostra Signora della Guardia, a chapel
consecrated in 1922, marks the summit of the pass but the
medieval pilgrim hospice has gone. The arch to the right of
the church is the 'Gateway to Tuscany' as the Cisa Pass lies
on the border with the province of Emiglia-Romagna.

Carrara is not directly on the route of the Via Francigena but, as the source of the world's finest marble is but a few kilometres away in the Apuan Alps of northern Tuscany, how could one not be tempted into a leisurely stopover after the long and exhausting trek down from the Cisa Pass? It is extraordinary to think that marble has been extracted here for architecture and art since the time of Ancient Rome and as yet, there is not the slightest hint of concern from within the industry that this priceless natural resource is in danger of being quarried to exhaustion. The name of Renaissance artist and sculptor Michelangelo Buonarotti (1475–1564) is synonymous with the medium of marble as two of the world's greatest sculpted works of art, *David* and *Pietà* were crafted by his hammer and chisel. When viewing the *Pietà*, it is impossible to equate the flowing lines of Mary's robe and her expression of anguished resignation with a solid lump of limestone. It was the artist himself who said that there is a statue already lodged in every block of stone and it was his responsibility to release it.

There are two main quarrying centres located above Carrara, whose duomo *(opposite)* is clad entirely in shimmering marble. The Frantiscritti and Colonnata quarries are both accessible by road and visible to independent travellers but there are local tour companies who take visitors into the heart of the quarries in four-wheel-drive vehicles. It is extraordinary to see at close quarters just how big the extracted blocks of marble are, something only made possible by the latest techniques involving the use of diamond-encrusted wire to cut the rock with perfect precision. The giant stones are then taken down to the coast for processing or shipping out to other parts of the world. It all seems a far cry from when the Romans used manual labour (a lot of it) and extraction techniques that involved driving fig wood stakes into natural fissures in the rock, and soaking the wood so that natural expansion caused the detachment of the stone block. Not every seam of marble around Carrara is of the almost pure white *statuario* quality and it is fascinating to see how nature has contrived to create natural shading and colouring *(overleaf)* by introducing sand or various minerals into the rock strata.

Great St Bernard
Pass
Aosta
Pavia
Lucca
Siena
Rome

VIA FRANCIGENA 237

Oh what a difference a day makes! I made the mistake of arriving in Lucca on a late summer Sunday afternoon and the walled city's narrow streets were more tightly packed than a London Underground platform during rush hour. On the following morning I had the place to myself and was fully able to savour the architectural treasures of the city.

Lucca was colonized by Rome during the early second century BC and still retains the layout of a Roman military encampment with streets intersecting at right angles along each side of the two main thoroughfares. Between the twelfth and fourteenth centuries Lucca flourished economically by manufacturing and trading in silk, exporting it throughout Europe and the Orient. This accrued wealth resulted in a church rebuilding programme, and some of the merchants and leading figures of that period ploughed their wealth into imposing Gothic residences, some of which have retained their original towers. One such important local was Paolo Guinigi, Lord of Lucca in 1400, whose tower house, the Torre Guinigi *(opposite, above left)* is one of the city's most prominent landmarks. The 135ft (41m) red brick tower was one of the last to continue the Italian tradition of planting oak trees on the top and visitors who manage to climb the 230 steps then have to squeeze their way around tree roots and branches. Lucca's main square, the Piazza San Michele evolved from the original Roman forum and is named after the magnificent church of San Michele in Foro, whose exceptionally tall thirteenth-century façade of twisted marble columns *(opposite, above right)* is an exquisite example of Pisan Romanesque architecture. The city's cathedral, the Duomo di San Martino lacks the flamboyance of San Michele but nevertheless its façade of alternating green and white marble by thirteenth-century architect Guidetto da Como *(opposite, below)* is yet another example of how the subtleties of colour within a naturally occurring stone can be harnessed in such a creative manner. The 2½ miles (4km) of vast ramparts still completely encircling the city took almost a century and half to complete. Work on the defensive perimeter began in 1600 and included four gates and eleven projecting bastions. A fifth gate was added at the beginning of the nineteenth century and the walls were subsequently planted with two rows of trees to create a unique elevated public park for both pedestrians and cyclists.

San Gimignano's thirteen surviving towers reflect the
town's past importance and wealth dating back to the
early-fourteenth century when there were seventy-two such
structures dominating the surrounding Tuscan countryside.
Although primarily built as status symbols, the towers
were also inhabited and their thick walls offered a cool
space during the heat of summer and insulation in winter.
According to legend the town originated as an Etruscan
settlement, but its documented history began in 929 when
established as market town that subsequently benefited from
its location on the Via Francigena. San Gimignano was listed
as a World Heritage Site in 1990.

Siena is the embodiment of a medieval city and has remarkably managed to retain most of the Gothic architectural influences that prevailed between the twelfth and fifteenth centuries. Its present-day state of conservation is a rare phenomenon that can be attributed to several factors including the Black Death, the plague that decimated Europe and in 1348 reduced Siena's population of 100,000 by two thirds. The period of decline that followed became a centuries-long economic slump and this meant little or no further development took place to 'upgrade' the magnificent Gothic architecture of the city's earlier golden era of prosperity. Siena is set amid the majestic landscapes of central Tuscany and although the site was settled in pre-Roman times, it was the establishing of a military colony named *Saena Julia* in the first century BC that laid the foundations for the city that exists today. Siena was developed over three hills connected by streets in a Y-shape and the city's main public square, the Piazza del Campo was created at the central intersection. The sloping fan-shaped piazza was originally the site of a Roman market place and is renowned worldwide for staging the historic Palio horse race, competed for by the city's seventeen *contrade* (districts or parishes). The cathedral is one of Italy's finest and the colour, style and detail of the west front is just incredible but it is extraordinary

Great St Bernard
Pass
Pavia
Siena
Aosta
Lucca
Rome

VIA FRANCIGENA 241

to think that Siena's intense rivalry with nearby Florence almost resulted in the perfect church we see today being replaced by something vast, so big in fact that the current building would have been just one of the mega-cathedral's transepts! The interior of the duomo *(below)* is just as exquisitely beautiful as the exterior; the roof vault is supported on black and white pillars and details such as the carved font by Nicola Pisano, the vast inlaid marble floor and the Piccolomini Library are just some of the architectural masterpieces to savour. Standing directly opposite the cathedral's west front is Santa Maria della Scala, a former medieval hospital now open as a cultural centre and museum of art, history and archaeology with particular emphasis on the legacy of caring for pilgrims on the Via Francigena. Siena's duomo is an imposing sight up close but possibly even more so when seen from a distance *(overleaf)* when its true stature can be fully appreciated.

The mighty basilica of San Paulo fuori le Mura (St Paul Outside-the-Walls) stands on the site where he was buried after his martyrdom. Most of the main roads outside the walls of ancient Rome were lined with tombs and burial sites and St Paul was buried in the necropolis alongside the Via Ostiense. The precise date of the apostle's martyrdom is uncertain but he possibly shared St Peter's fate by being caught up in Nero's vindictive persecution of Christians as though the great fire of AD 64 that destroyed much of Rome were their fault. St Paul's tomb was initially marked by a small Christian shrine but during the early part of the fourth century he was afforded the same honour as St Peter when Emperor Constantine built a basilica on that site. It soon became such a popular place of pilgrimage that a much larger church was needed and the magnificent replacement allegedly exceeded the size and grandeur of St Peter's. Despite being sacked in the eighth and ninth centuries, surviving a twelfth-century fire and the flooding of the Tiber in 1700, the basilica just about kept going until 1823 when it was almost completely destroyed by a huge fire. Fortunately, some frescoes, mosaics and paintings were saved but whoever was tasked with rebuilding the basilica would be presented with a virtually blank canvas. That responsibility fell to a specialist in Neoclassical architecture, Luigi Poletti (1792–1869) who vowed to reconstruct an exact replica of the original. He kept that promise and the new basilica *(opposite)* was consecrated by Pope Pius IX in December 1854. Nothing can prepare you for the sight of the 440ft (135m) nave with double flanking aisles, each separated by four rows of twenty granite columns leading up to a richly decorated gold-coffered ceiling. However, from the perspective of the basilica as a place of pilgrimage, the greatest treasure of San Paulo was discovered during archaeological work carried out at the beginning of the twenty-first century beneath the papal altar.

The sarcophagus of the apostle has been revealed exactly in the place where the Emperor Constantine had the first altar built and sitting just above the tomb of unpolished marble, a Latin inscription reads *PAULO APOSTOLO MART* (Paul Apostle Martyr). The ancient apse of that original basilica containing the tomb has also been uncovered and a section is also now visible beneath a sheet of reinforced glass.

The glorious cloister of the Benedictine abbey at San
Paulo *(left)* miraculously survived the great fire of 1823
that destroyed most of the church. The paired columns
of twisted marble were created between 1205–35 by one
of Rome's renowned Cosmati, a family of artists spanning
four generations from the twelfth century onwards who
specialized in mosaic inlay. The work at San Paolo was
attributed to Giovanni Cosmati. *(Right)* Santo Spirito in
Sassia was originally founded by King Ine of Wessex as a
church and hospice for Saxon pilgrims and was the first of
Rome's churches visited by Sigeric after St Peter's.

Following his conversion to Christianity during the early part of the fourth century, the Roman Emperor Constantine initiated the building of a church over the tomb of the martyred apostle, St Peter. It was consecrated in AD 326 and Constantine's basilica survived centuries of sacking and pillaging by marauding Barbarian tribes. It witnessed the solemn coronation of Holy Roman Emperors such as Charlemagne (Christmas Day, AD 800) and evolved into an important place of Christian pilgrimage. However, by the mid-fifteenth century, time had taken its toll and despite having been repaired, restored and renovated the building was in serious decline. In 1452 Pope Nicholas V had proposed a significant rebuilding programme based upon a cruciform plan with a dome and a new choir but he died just three years later and his more indecisive successors opted to continue with the 'patch up and pray' approach. Almost fifty years elapsed until Pope Julius II in 1503 made a concerted attempt to address the issue but as both he and his architect Donato Bramante (1444–1514) died less than a decade later, the plans were once again the subject of much arguing and wrangling among the Papacy and architectural elite of Rome. The chaos and uncertainty was finally brought to an end in 1547 when Pope Paul III appointed Michelangelo to sort out the mess. The seventy-two-year-old sculptor was already chief architect to the Vatican at that time and elected to return to Bramante's original Greek cruciform plan but with a significantly higher dome *(opposite, above)*. Work progressed up to and well beyond Michelangelo's death in 1564 and by the end of that century, the apse, dome and transepts had been completed. Although the interior of St Peter's is vast, there is no sense whatsoever of a cold, cavernous space because all the architects, sculptors and painters have ultimately worked in harmony to produce a combination of statuary, furnishings and colours that works so well. The masterstroke and unifying feature must be Bernini's glorious *baldacchino (opposite, below)*, whose twisted and gilded bronze columns soar upwards to the elaborate canopy covering the papal altar set above St Peter's tomb. However, Bernini's genius was not confined to the interior and his layout and design of St Peter's Square were truly inspirational. The gently curving colonnades achieved this and they also served as a metaphorical pair of welcoming arms, beckoning pilgrims into the church.

Michelangelo's *Pietà (above)* is arguably the world's most expressive and moving piece of religious sculpture and the first monument encountered by visitors to the interior of St Peter's Basilica. The work was carved between 1498–1500 from a single block of Carrara marble. There are no tears of grief, simply an aura of questioning resignation so perfectly represented by the fingers of her outstretched hand. *(Opposite)* Michelangelo was also largely responsible for the design of St Peter's magnificent dome.

INDEX

FURTHER DETAILS

The organizations listed below may be helpful to anyone seeking further information about the pilgrimage routes or other significant places featured in the book.

ST CUTHBERT'S WAY
www.stcuthbertsway.info

ST WINEFRIDE'S WELL
www.saintwinefrideswell.com
john.laiguille@btconnect.com

THE PILGRIMS WAY
www.pilgrimswaycanterbury.org
enquiries@canterbury-cathedral.org

LES CHEMINS DU MONT-SAINT-MICHEL
www.lescheminsdumontsaintmichel.com
chemins-st-michel@wanadoo.fr

VIA PODIENSIS / CAMINO FRANCÉS / VIA DE LA PLATA
www.csj.org.uk

VIA COLONIENSIS / MÜNCHNER JAKOBSWEG
www.deutsche-jakobus-gesellschaft.de
info@deutsche-jakobus-gesellschaft.de

VIA DI FRANCESCO
www.viadifrancesco.it
www.laverna.it

VIA FRANCIGENA
www.viefrancigene.org

ACKNOWLEDGMENTS

My sincere thanks to Arianna Osti for her brilliant design and an intuitive final picture selection that has perfectly encapsulated the atmosphere, architecture and landscapes of the pilgrimage routes.

My appreciation also to Andrew Dunn and publishers Frances Lincoln for their longstanding and unwavering commitment to the increasingly 'at risk species' of illustrated non-fiction.